SPEAK THE ANSWER, NOT THE PROBLEM

YVONNE PERKINS

Published 2025
Printed in the United States of America

First Edition
ISBN (softcover): 978-1-963380-XX-X
ISBN (e-book): 978-1-963380-XX-X

For information, address:
Holzer Books LLC
8 The Green, Ste. A
Dover, Delaware 19901 USA

For information about special discounts available for bulk purchases, sales promotions, and educational needs, contact:
info@holzerbooksllc.com
+1 (888) 901-7776

Scripture quotations from The Authorized (King James) Version. Rights in the Authorized Version in the United Kingdom are vested in the Crown. Reproduced by permission of the Crown's patentee, Cambridge University Press

holzerbooksLLC©

CONTENTS

This book is dedicated to **Prophetess Vickie Pendleton**.

While serving as one of the armor bearers under Prophetess Rose Mary Blackwell, I was given the assignment to respond to the prayer requests submitted to *Standing in the Gap Ministries*.

Recently, while sorting through thousands of old emails (don't judge me!), I came across a message from **Evangelist Vickie Pendleton** that stopped me in my tracks. It read:

"I am moved by each anointed prayer you send out. Think of how you can publish your prayers and meditations. You have covered so many topics and could keep the parties anonymous. But these anointed prayers must be available for others. They would guide so many in how to pray for specific situations!"

That was nearly twenty years ago.

Prophetess Vickie, I finally did it.

FOREWORD
BY ELDER CYNTHIA BRIDGES

Intercessor Dr. Yvonne's newest book, *Speak The Answer, Not The Problem*, was birthed out of the prayer training under Prophetess Rose Mary Blackwell's Standing in the Gap Ministries (SITG). Dr. Yvonne, myself, and many intercessors from various churches participated in the training at Monday Night Prayer and Monthly Saturday Prayer. Those services were full of fiery, Spirit-led instruction and demonstration.

We were taught not to pray about the problem, for God already knew the situation! Instead, we were instructed to find the answer to the problem in the Bible. Then, by faith and authority, we were to speak it out in prayer. Dr. Yvonne's book reflects this prayer training! She provides the prayer concern, scripture references, and the prayer answer—making it a valuable resource for both the novice and the mature intercessor.

I am grateful that Dr. Yvonne obeyed the Lord and completed this book! It is such a strategic book that will help activate and sharpen every intercessor.

In His Service,
Elder Cynthia Bridges

FOREWORD

BY PROPHETESS LILLY JONES

In a world inundated with challenges, negativity, and uncertainty, it is easy to find ourselves speaking more about our problems than the solutions God has already provided. *Speak The Answer, Not The Problem* serves as a powerful guide to shift our mindset and words to align with God's truth, offering hope and practical steps to overcome life's obstacles.

Each chapter challenges us to look beyond the visible and trust in the unseen, reminding us of 2 Corinthians 5:7:

"For we live by faith, not by sight."

Whether you're navigating personal trials, relationships, or professional challenges, the lessons within these pages will inspire you to see every problem as an opportunity to speak God's solution into existence.

Dr. Yvonne Perkins masterfully combines biblical principles with practical application, showing us how to live out Romans 12:2:

"Do not conform to the pattern of this world, but be transformed by the renewing of your mind."

This book isn't just a tool; it's a roadmap for anyone ready to move from struggle to victory by the power of faith-filled words.

Prepare your heart and mind to experience a transformation as you begin to speak God's answers over your life. This is more than a book; it's a call to action, a faith-filled declaration, and a reminder that with God, all things are possible.

Dear Friend and Co-Laborer in Christ,

Prophetess Lilly Jones

FOREWORD
BY EVG. JACQUELINE MARSHALL

Speak The Answer, Not The Problem is more than a book—it is a step-by-step handbook written to equip, empower, and educate you on the basic principles of intercession. Dr. Yvonne takes great care throughout the book to relate scripture references to everything being taught. These guided, scripture-based prayers will assist you in increasing your prayer language and expertise as an intercessor.

Each example will inspire and encourage you not only to read the book but to apply the impactful principles to your personal life, church, community, and the world as a whole—advancing the Kingdom of God!

If you are looking for the *secret sauce* to a spiritual breakthrough, learning how to speak the answers to your problems, and making a life-changing impact on the earth, I highly recommend this book!

Evg. Jacqueline Marshall

Author, *Becoming A Woman of Wholeness, New Season, New You*

How to Get Answers from God

You must believe that God is God. You must believe that God is omnipotent. Webster defines *omnipotent* as "one who has unlimited power or authority" and "having virtually unlimited authority or influence." You must believe that God is omnipresent and has the ability to be everywhere all at once. *Omniscience* is defined as "having infinite awareness, understanding, and insight" and "the state of having total knowledge; the quality of knowing everything."

If you desire God to answer your prayers, you must believe Hebrews 11:6: "But without faith it is impossible to please him: for he that cometh to God must believe that he is, and that he is a rewarder of them that diligently seek him."

You must ask. Yes, God is all-knowing, all-seeing, and ever-present, but he instructs you to ask.

James 1:5: "If any of you lack wisdom, let him ask of God, that giveth to all men liberally, and upbraideth not; and it shall be given him."

Luke 11:9–10: "And I say unto you, Ask, and it shall be given you; seek, and ye shall find; knock, and it shall be opened unto you. For every one that asketh receiveth; and he that seeketh findeth; and to him that knocketh it shall be opened."

Matthew 7:7–8: "Ask, and keep on asking, and it will be given to you; seek, and keep on seeking, and you will find it. Knock, and keep on knocking, and the door will be opened to you. For everyone who keeps on asking receives, and he who keeps on seeking finds, and to him who keeps on knocking, it will be opened."

Matthew 18:19: "Again I say unto you, That if two of you shall agree on earth as touching anything that they shall ask, it shall be done for them of my Father which is in heaven."

John 14:13–14: "And whatsoever ye shall ask in my name, that will I do, that the Father may be glorified in the Son. If ye shall ask anything in my name, I will do it."

Hebrews 4:6: "Let us therefore come boldly unto the throne of grace, that we may obtain mercy, and find grace to help in time of need."

James 4:3: "Ye ask, and receive not, because ye ask amiss, that ye may consume it upon your lusts."

Matthew 5:23–24: "Therefore if thou bring thy gift to the altar, and there rememberest that thy brother hath ought against thee; leave there thy gift before the altar, and go thy way; first be reconciled to thy brother, and then come and offer thy gift."

Psalm 32:1–2: "Blessed is he whose transgression is forgiven, whose sin is covered. Blessed is the man unto whom the Lord imputeth not iniquity, and in whose spirit there is no guile."

Isaiah 59:1–3: "Behold, the Lord's hand is not shortened, that it cannot save; neither his ear heavy, that it cannot hear: but your iniquities have separated between you and your God, and your sins have hid his face from you, that he will not hear. For your hands are defiled with blood, and your fingers with iniquity; your lips have spoken lies, your tongue hath muttered perverseness."

God is ready to answer your prayers. Ask him. Check your heart and motives. Believe it is his will and delight to answer your prayers.

One more thing: Satan will fight you on every level to get you to doubt—to convince you that God does not hear, does not care, and will not answer you. Stand firm in the Word of God and refuse to doubt. You must have unshakable faith—faith that says, *I don't care what it looks like, what it sounds like, or what anyone else says if it contradicts what I know God says.*

In my profession as a clinical therapist, I worked with a population of in-patient mentally ill clients. Sometimes I encountered clients who had a "fixation" on a person, place, or thing. You could not convince that person of anything other than what they believed, regardless of what evidence you presented to them.

When I am praying for something that seems like it will not be, I pray that God will let me have a fixation on the answer. My faith will hold fast, and I will not be persuaded of anything else but that God will and is answering my prayer. I am crazy enough to believe God will do just what he says.

Acts 27:25: "Wherefore, sirs, be of good cheer: for I believe God, that it shall be even as it was told me."

Romans 4:16–22: "Therefore it is of faith, that it might be by grace; to the end the promise might be sure to all the seed; not to that only which is of the law, but to that also which is of the faith of Abraham, who is the father of us all (as it is written, I have made thee a father of many nations) before him whom he believed, even God, who quickeneth the dead, and calleth those things which be not as though they were. Who against hope believed in hope, that he might become the father of many nations, according to that which was spoken, So shall thy seed be. And being not weak in faith, he considered not his own body now dead, when he was about an hundred years old, neither yet the deadness of Sarah's womb. He staggered not at the promise of God through unbelief; but was strong in faith, giving glory to God, and being fully persuaded that what he had promised, he was able also to perform. And therefore it was imputed to him for righteousness."

Identify the Problem

You cannot solve a problem until you identify it. You cannot identify that problem when you are emotional. If you are struggling with an issue, you should take the time to deal with it when you are calm.

These are steps I think will be helpful:

1. Find a quiet place where you will not be disturbed.

2. Anoint yourself with oil.

3. Have your Bible at your side and spend time in worship.

Worship will prepare your heart to hear from God.

Set the atmosphere for worship by listening to worship music. Bring in your mind and thoughts to focus on the goodness of God. At this stage, you are not presenting the problem to God but are in a posture of loving him, adoring him, and trusting him. You are in a place of gratitude. Do not rush through this stage. Wait quietly in his presence.

Now talk to God about the situation you are dealing with. You can be perfectly honest with God about your feelings because he will not judge you—he knows anyway. In other words, you can tell God if you are angry, hurt, or disappointed—whatever it is. Ask for his direction and wisdom, and then **listen** for his response.

Ask the Holy Spirit, *What is the answer? What is the word that I need to stand on?* This is the method I use, and God has never failed to provide the answer.

The internet is a good resource for quickly finding scriptures. You can Google phrases like *Show me scriptures about anger* or *building my faith* or *trusting God.* Do not hesitate to use any method available to you.

LOOK FOR THE ANSWER

Identify the problem and ask the Holy Spirit for the answer. As a believer, and particularly as an intercessor, it is imperative that you understand the operation and purpose of the Holy Spirit. You do not operate as a lone ranger. **Regardless** of how many degrees you have—secular or nonsecular—you must always be dependent on the Word of God.

How do you look for the answer?

- **John 14:25–27**: "All this I have spoken while still with you. But the Advocate, the Holy Spirit, whom the Father will send in my name, will teach you all things and will remind you of everything I have said to you. Peace I leave with you; my peace I give you. I do not give to you as the world gives. Do not let your hearts be troubled and do not be afraid."

- **Proverbs 3:5–7**: "Trust in the Lord with all thine heart; and lean not unto thine own understanding. In all thy ways acknowledge him, and he shall direct thy paths. Be not wise in thine own eyes:

fear the Lord, and depart from evil."

- **James 1:5–6**: "If any of you lacks wisdom, let him ask of God, who gives to all liberally and without reproach, and it will be given to him. But let him ask in faith, with no doubting, for he who doubts is like a wave of the sea driven and tossed by the wind."

- **Mark 11:24**: "Therefore I say unto you, What things soever ye desire, when ye pray, believe that ye receive them, and ye shall have them."

- **Matthew 7:7–8**: "Ask, and it shall be given you; seek, and ye shall find; knock, and it shall be opened unto you. For every one that asketh receiveth; and he that seeketh findeth; and to him that knocketh it shall be opened."

- **Isaiah 30:21**: "And thine ears shall hear a word behind thee, saying, This is the way, walk ye in it, when ye turn to the right hand, and when ye turn to the left."

How do you look for the answer? **Prepare your mind** to seek the answer. **Prepare your spirit** to receive the answer by setting the atmosphere to hear from God—for example, by finding a quiet place, anointing yourself with blessed oil, and playing worship music to bring your mind, body, and spirit into alignment with the Holy Spirit. Quiet yourself and prepare to listen for the voice of God.

FAITH COMES BY HEARING

Faith comes by hearing. Many times, we interpret this to mean hearing the preacher preach the Word of God. It is true that God uses men and women of God to release a *rhema* word to us by preaching or ministering the Word of God. Do you not know that when you speak out loud, the sound travels outside of your body and returns to you?

According to the **National Institute on Deafness and Other Communication Disorders (NIDCD),** when we hear a sound, sound waves enter the outer ear and travel through the ear canal, causing the eardrum to vibrate. These vibrations are then amplified by tiny bones in the middle ear, which send the sound waves to the fluid-filled cochlea in the inner ear. Hair cells convert the vibrations into electrical signals that are carried by the auditory nerve to the brain, which interprets the signals as sound. You speak, and then you hear what you spoke.

It is good practice to read the Word of God out loud. It is good practice to pray out loud, even when you are home alone. Why? I learned during my time training intercessors that many are afraid of their own voice. I teach them that Satan is afraid of their voice, which is why they must take every opportunity to pray out loud. This is a method to build up your faith as you declare the Word of God to yourself. You are reinforcing the Word of God in your inner man.

Say what God says about you. Say what he says about situations and circumstances. Release it into the atmosphere (air), geosphere (land), biosphere (living things), and hydrosphere (water). Let the heavens and Satan hear you declare the Word of God. You must study and meditate on the Word of God. You cannot declare that which you do not know. When you know *what you know that you know*—that it is so—you can stand on that Word.

Trust the Word of God. When God spoke, things happened. When God declared, "Let it be," it became. God has given us power to declare and decree his Word. His Word will never fail to produce or manifest the things of God. We speak his Word, and it becomes reality.

- **Jeremiah 1:12**: "Then said the Lord unto me, Thou hast well seen: for I will hasten my word to perform it."

- **Psalm 32:8**: "I will instruct you and teach you in the way you should go; I will counsel you with my loving eye on you."

- **Psalm 37:23–24**: "The Lord makes firm the steps of the one who delights in him; though he may stumble, he will not fall, for the Lord upholds him with his hand."

- **Matthew 24:35**: "Heaven and earth shall pass away, but my words shall not pass away."

Trust God's love and compassion for you:

- **Isaiah 54:10**: "For the mountains shall depart, and the hills be removed; but my kindness shall not depart from thee, neither shall the covenant of my peace be removed, saith the Lord that hath mercy on thee."

- **Jeremiah 29:11**: "For I know the thoughts that I think toward you, saith the Lord, thoughts of peace, and not of evil, to give you an expected end."

TRUST GOD

Faith comes by hearing and hearing by the Word of God. This does not only refer to what you hear from the pulpit. When you confess the Word of God out loud, you release a sound into the atmosphere, and that sound comes back into your spirit.

- **Romans 10:8–9**: "But what saith it? The word is nigh thee, even in thy mouth, and in thy heart: that is, the word of faith, which we preach; that if thou shalt confess with thy mouth the Lord Jesus, and shalt believe in thine heart that God hath raised him from the dead, thou shalt be saved."

- **Romans 10:17**: "So then faith cometh by hearing, and hearing by the word of God."

Unshakeable faith. I worked at Jackson Park Hospital as a clinical therapist and had never received a raise. The corporate employees received a raise each year but stated there was no money in the budget for the staff. The package included sick days, but you had to bring in a medical statement for even one sick day. I was even hurt on the job while dealing with clients who were fighting, and I had to fight for time off to recover. *Whew.*

I began seeking God for a new job. I began to confess this daily:

Psalm 5:11–12: "But let all those that put their trust in thee rejoice: let them ever shout for joy, because thou defendest them: let them also that love thy name be joyful in thee. For thou, Lord, wilt bless the righteous; with favour wilt thou compass him as with a shield."

I confessed this daily for 30 days: *God, I rejoice in you, and I thank you that your favor surrounds me and that I have a job with good benefits in the field that I desire. I CONFESSED THE WORD OF GOD.*

I received that new job.

But wait. Jackson Park Hospital only paid me for half of my sick days when I left. I received two weeks of paid vacation as part of their benefits package.

Well, God gave me a job that I did not qualify for. The job was for an LCPC position, but I did not qualify because I did not have enough time as an LPC to even be able to take that exam. You are required to be in the LPC position for two years before you can take the test for the LCPC (*Licensed Clinical Professional Counselor*).

I was hired as an LCPC with the stipulation that I had one year to take and pass the exam. In the meantime, I received pay as an LCPC.

But wait.

The benefits package included **twelve sick days, three personal days, and three paid weeks of vacation.**

This is what happens when you have **unshakable faith.**

WRITE THE ANSWER

SPEAK THE ANSWER NOT THE PROBLEM.

THE ANSWER IS THE WORD OF GOD.

God, you are your Word. The Bible is so relevant to our day-to-day life. It contains answers to everything we will face in life.

Do you have problems with your marriage? Are you single? Do you have issues with family relationships? Do you need financial help? Have you been abused? Do you need a job? Are your children rebellious? The answer is in the Word of God.

Write it out.

One of my assignments from Prophetess Rose Mary Blackwell (*Standing in the Gap Ministry*) was to respond to the different prayer requests that were sent in. I could not respond to these requests according to my understanding, thoughts, or opinions. I would anoint myself with oil and pray for the leading of the Holy Spirit as I read the request. The Holy Spirit would lead me to the appropriate scriptures.

This is where I first started using the term **"Speak the answer, not the problem. The answer is the Word of God."**

Some situations seem to be ongoing attacks. Ask the Holy Spirit to take you to the Word that applies. Write out your prayer using the scriptures that the Holy Spirit gives you. Print it out and place it where you can easily see it. Read it out loud. **Decree and declare.**

You write the answer by **decreeing and declaring** what God says about the situation and confessing your belief in His Word. I don't find it necessary to write out every scripture. Instead, I write a statement declaring what God's Word says He will do. I write it out and post it somewhere I can see it often. I confess it out loud. Sometimes I just walk by the note, read it, place my hand on it, and confess the truth of what I have written.

Ask the Holy Spirit to teach you how to pray for this situation. What scriptures are you standing on to defeat the enemy? What is God saying through His Word?

PRAY IN THE HOLY SPIRIT. Use your heavenly language. God has given it to us, and it has a purpose.

I know someone is saying, *I can't just pray like that.* The Bible says:

> **Acts 2:3–4**: "And there appeared unto them cloven tongues like as of fire, and it sat upon each of them. And they were all filled with the Holy Ghost and began to speak with other tongues, as the Spirit gave them utterance."

Yes, the Bible also says:

> **Romans 8:26**: "Likewise the Spirit also helpeth our infirmities: for we know not what we should pray for as we ought: but the Spirit itself maketh intercession for us with groanings which cannot be uttered."

A decree is taking God's words and speaking them out. You are giving God His words back to Him.

We have been given the authority from Jesus to make these decrees into our realms of influence. As we do this, we begin to create the will of God in our life in the spiritual realm. We hold the royal scepter of authority. We have been given the power to **bind and loose**, to declare **what will and will not be.**

Job 22:28: "Thou shalt also decree a thing, and it shall be established unto thee: and the light shall shine upon thy ways."

What is a decree?

Webster defines it this way:

1. An order usually having the force of law

2. A religious ordinance enacted by a council or titular head

3. A foreordaining will

In other words, a decree is an **official order issued by a legal authority.**

A decree carries the **weight of a court order.** The decree starts with a statement of **what will happen.** The decree institutes the power, will, and purpose of God.

Decrees post a judgment against the enemy.

• It gives us favor against the enemy.

• The enemy has no power to change our decree.

• Decrees align us with God's words.

This is where you use your faith to bring forth decrees in your life. **Faith enables us to see what is unseen and cause it to come forth.** At the same time, it allows us to see what is and declare **it will not be.**

We use our mouths to speak things into our reality.

We decree:

• Our household is saved.

• Our marriages are strong.

• We have more than enough.

To make a decree, you must have the legal authority to do so. **We have been given the authority from Jesus** to make decrees with the expectation that they shall be established in our lives.

To **declare** means **to make something known formally and officially.** What good would a decree be if it was not made known to others?

A **declaration** is defined as making an announcement, making something known, or an affirmation that something is true.

I decree and declare the Word of God is my truth.

It is an announcement to Satan: **I will not back down but stand and declare my faith in God.**

Can you make any type of decree you wish and expect God to back you up? **No.**

Your decree must **line up with the Word of God.** A decree is taking God's Word and speaking it out loud. Issuing a decree is not based on **your words, thoughts, desires, or wishes.** The decree must be based on the foundational truth of God's Word.

That is why **He, God, will establish it.** It is **His own words.**

When we return God's Word to Him, **angels are released to carry out the fulfillment of the scripture.**

Example of a Written Prayer

SPEAK THE ANSWER, NOT THE PROBLEM.

THE ANSWER IS THE WORD OF GOD.

Heavenly Father, we come in the name of your Son, Jesus, on behalf of our children. We ask that you cover them in the blood of Jesus from the crown of their heads to the soles of their feet. We pray that you give them good health and heal them from disease and infirmity.

We decree and declare that they present their bodies as a living sacrifice to you. They understand that their bodies are your temple and that you have purchased them with your blood. Therefore, they honor their bodies, they flee youthful lusts, and drugs, alcohol, and cigarettes shall not touch their lips. Their bodies will not receive them but reject them.

We plant the seed of righteousness in them and decree that it shall prosper and take root in them, and they shall be rooted and grounded in your Word. Our children are facing a society that embraces perverse ideas and lifestyles. We decree and declare that every girl will be a woman, and every boy will be a man, and they shall embrace the image in which you created them. Your blood and holy Word preserve them, and we block every attack of the enemy in their mind, body, spirit, and soul. We cast down every imagination that says otherwise, bring it into captivity, and cause them to line up with your Word.

Your Word declares:

Ephesians 6:1–2: "Children, obey your parents in the Lord: for this is right. Honour thy father and mother; which is the first commandment with promise."

So we bind up the spirit of rebellion in them and loose the spirit of obedience into their lives. Your Word teaches us not to provoke them to anger but to train, nurture, and love them. We pray for wisdom to know how to reach them. Give us words that they will hear. Let us show them by example how to love and fear you. Teach us how to discipline without abuse but to discipline in love through training, teaching, correcting, and redirecting them in the right way. Show us the better way to meet their needs as their parents—not as their friends, but as those who guide and parent them.

We decree that our children shall be taught of you, and great shall be their peace.

> **Isaiah 54:13–14**: "And all thy children shall be taught of the Lord, and great shall be the peace of thy children. In righteousness shalt thou be established: thou shalt be far from oppression; for thou shalt not fear: and from terror; for it shall not come near thee."

We decree that all of our children, grandchildren, nieces, nephews, and cousins shall live in peace. Peace surrounds them as they travel to and from school, in school, and wherever they gather. Even as Rachel cried out for her children, we cry out for our children, for the blood has indeed come up to the windows and the blood of the innocent runs in the street

We bind up violence, anger, rage, and terror, and it shall not come near them. Your blood is a wall between them and the rapist, drug dealer, gangs, terrorists, cults, and false religions. You preserve them from the road of destruction.

You have set before them life and death, and they choose life. They will love you with all their might, heart, and mind. They shall be God-chasers, pursuers of your heart, and they hear your voice, and another they will not follow. They love your law and delight in it, and they seek to please you. They are a generation that shall rise up and declare your goodness. You shall use them greatly.

We pray for our children who live in chaotic situations, that you will protect them and keep them safe from hurt and harm. We pray for those who are being raised by grandparents or other relatives because their parents are caught up in drugs or in prison. We bind up the spirits of rejection, anger, hatred, and bitterness. Your Word declares:

Romans 8:28: "And we know that all things work together for good to them that love God, to them who are the called according to his purpose."

Work out your will in their lives.

We pray for those who have lost parents due to tragedy or death, that they will experience your love and care, for you are a mother to the motherless and a father to the fatherless.

We decree and declare victory in their lives. They have favor in school, with peers, and with teachers. They are the best of the best. You open up their abilities to soak up knowledge like a sponge. They are creative. Our children are entrepreneurs, designers, inventors, teachers, lawyers, doctors, and financial masters. Our children are sensitive, kind, compassionate, and giving. They are the head and not the tail. They excel in everything they put their hands to do.

They shall not forget you but remember you in their youth.

They shall remember that it is you who has given them favor, gifts, and talents to get wealth, and they shall always give you the glory. Every skill and gift you give them shall be for your glory.

Bind their feet to the path of righteousness, clothe them in sanctification, and perfume them with holiness. Saturate them in your love. Enlighten their eyes and open up their understanding.

We draw the bloodline around them, under them, and through them, and we make a **bold declaration** that **Satan will not have them.**

We will never give up on them. We will never let them go. They belong to you, and we commit them into your hands.

We ask that you send **warring angels** to walk with them, **ministering angels** to be with them, and that you be a fence all around them.

We give you praise in advance for how you are keeping them, loving them, and protecting them.

We speak over their lives that they shall be **greatly used by you.**

Find the scripture references in this prayer and write it down.

Prayer for Marriages

SPEAK THE ANSWER, NOT THE PROBLEM.

THE ANSWER IS THE WORD OF GOD.

God established marriage and called it honorable. Satan tries to destroy everything that God created. I have responded to many regarding marriage issues. In this section, I have combined and rewritten some of those responses.

Father God, I plead the **blood of Jesus** over every couple—their home, marriage, emotions, finances, family, and every connection to them. I superimpose the will of God over the purpose of the enemy and **cancel his assignment and plans.**

Your Word warns us:

1 Peter 5:8: "Be sober, be vigilant; because your adversary the devil, as a roaring lion, walketh about, seeking whom he may devour."

I declare that these couples recognize this as a spiritual attack from the enemy, who wants to destroy the very institution that you have sanctioned.

I bind up every spirit of hurt, pain, rejection, pride, bitterness, unforgiveness, self-righteousness, ineffective communication, and lack of communication.

I loose the spirit of **unfailing love, understanding, peace, joy, compassion, forgiveness, humility, determination, strength, and hope.**

I speak **wholeness** to every area where the enemy has sent arrows of hurtful words spoken out of anger, jealousy, frustration, misunderstanding, and insensitivity. I ask you, the **Great Physician,** to go in and do open-heart surgery.

I speak **mind transformation, a spirit of repentance, and forgiveness.** May *agape* love cover each other's limitations and weaknesses. I speak that their hearts are **circumcised toward each other** so that they may see, understand, and perceive each other's pain.

I call forth **a renewal of love, desire, touching, and longing** for each other. I speak that they will be **examples to others** of what God can and will do when each humbles themselves before Him.

I declare their testimony will be: *We made it through. We survived the storm. Our love endured, and we are better than ever before. This time, our love is mature, wiser, and stronger.*

They are believers in your Word and know that even in this, **you have a purpose.** They understand that they must be tested so that they may tell others:

NOTHING IS TOO HARD FOR GOD.

Their ears are **closed** to those who speak negatively and **open** to hear your voice.

The enemy's purpose is **canceled.** They are **your servant and handmaiden** and will not tear each other down, nor will they allow anyone else to do so—for **they are one body.**

One body that needs your **healing touch.**

So, Father, I ask that you do what only **you can do**—mend these hearts together as a **threefold cord that will not be broken.**

Ecclesiastes 4:12: "And if one prevail against him, two shall withstand him; and a threefold cord is not quickly broken."

Enlighten their eyes that they may understand that **this is not about them, but about the enemy who comes to steal, kill, and destroy.**

Let them **come together in unity** and refuse to give the enemy the victory.

Shut the mouth of every **naysayer, onlooker, finger-pointer, and divisive spirit**—those who take sides and those who seek to separate and destroy.

I stand on your Word and stand fast in this **assignment** to cover spiritual leaders and the body of Christ. I **forbid the enemy** to take his prey.

I **disallow him this victory**—I **veto it in the name of the Father, Son, and Holy Ghost.**

I commission **warring angels** to destroy this enemy and **ministering angels** to minister to each heart.

I decree and declare that the **Holy Ghost, the Spirit of the Living God,** stands up in them and brings about **the spirit of reconciliation.**

I **break every contrary spirit** and **every spirit of pride** that would bring separation and cause them not to hear or heed your voice.

For you have declared:

> **Hebrews 13:4**: "Marriage is honourable in all, and the bed undefiled: but whoremongers and adulterers God will judge."

> **Genesis 2:24**: "Therefore shall a man leave his father and his mother, and shall cleave unto his wife: and they shall be one flesh."

I decree and declare that they shall **remember the vows made to you.**

They shall **stand.**

They shall **recover all.**

I declare that **the pursuit of love** shall take place and that **they shall overcome.**

*** *** ***

Scriptures for Meditation:

• **John 1:1**: "In the beginning was the Word, and the Word was with God, and the Word was God."

• **Exodus 12:13**: "And the blood shall be to you for a token upon the houses where ye are: and when I see the blood, I will pass over you, and the plague shall not be upon you to destroy you, when I smite the land of Egypt."

• **1 Peter 5:8**: "Be sober, be vigilant; because your adversary the devil, as a roaring lion, walketh about, seeking whom he may devour."

• **1 Corinthians 13:4–7**: "Charity suffereth long, and is kind; charity envieth not; charity vaunteth not itself, is not puffed up, doth not behave itself unseemly, seeketh not her own, is not easily provoked, thinketh no evil; rejoiceth not in iniquity, but rejoiceth in the truth; beareth all things, believeth all things, hopeth all things, endureth all things."

• **Colossians 3:14**: "And above all these things put on charity, which is the bond of perfectness."

• **Ephesians 4:32**: "And be ye kind one to another, tenderhearted, forgiving one another, even as God for Christ's sake hath forgiven you."

• **Mark 11:25**: "And when ye stand praying, forgive, if ye have ought against any: that your Father also which is in heaven may forgive you your trespasses."

• **Matthew 18:21–22**: "Then came Peter to him, and said, Lord, how oft shall my brother sin against me, and I forgive him? till seven times? Jesus saith unto him, I say not unto thee, Until seven times: but, Until seventy times seven."

• **Matthew 19:5**: "And said, For this cause shall a man leave father and mother, and shall cleave to his wife: and they twain shall be one flesh?"

• **Colossians 3:19**: "Husbands, love your wives, and be not bitter against them."

• **Ephesians 5:21–33**: A guide for love and submission in marriage.

Prayer For Children

SPEAK THE ANSWER, NOT THE PROBLEM.

THE ANSWER IS THE WORD OF GOD.

Heavenly Father, we come in the name of your Son, Jesus, on behalf of our children. We ask that you cover them in the **blood of Jesus** from the crown of their heads to the soles of their feet. We pray that you will give them good health and heal them from disease and infirmity.

We decree and declare that they present their bodies as a living sacrifice to you. They understand that their bodies are your temple and that you have purchased them with your blood. Therefore, they honor their bodies. They flee youthful lusts, and drugs, alcohol, and cigarettes shall not touch their lips. Their bodies will not receive them but reject them.

We plant the seed of righteousness in them and decree that it shall prosper and take root in them. They shall be **rooted and grounded** in your Word.

Our children are facing a society that embraces perverse ideas and lifestyles. We decree and declare that every girl will be a woman, and every boy will be a man, and they shall embrace the image in which you created them. Your blood and holy Word preserve them, and we block every attack of the enemy in their mind, body, spirit, and soul.

We cast down every imagination that says otherwise, bring it into captivity, and cause them to **line up with your Word.**

Your Word declares:

> **Ephesians 6:1–3**: "Children, obey your parents in the Lord: for this is right. Honour thy father and mother; which is the first commandment with promise; that it may be well with thee, and thou mayest live long on the earth."

So we bind up the **spirit of rebellion** in them and **loose the spirit of obedience** into their lives. Your Word teaches us **not to provoke them to anger** but to train, nurture, and love them.

We pray for wisdom to know how to reach them.

Give us words that they will hear.

Let us show them by example how to love and fear you.

Teach us how to discipline without abuse but to discipline in love through training, teaching, correcting, and redirecting them in the right way.

Show us the better way to meet their needs—as **their parents, not their friends,** but as those who **guide and parent them.**

We decree that our children shall be taught of you, and great shall be their peace.

> **Isaiah 54:13–14**: "And all thy children shall be taught of the Lord; and great shall be the peace of thy children. In righteousness shalt thou be established: thou shalt be far from oppression; for thou shalt not fear: and from terror; for it shall not come near thee."

We decree that all of our children, grandchildren, nieces, nephews, and cousins shall live in peace. Peace surrounds them as they travel to and from school, in school, and wherever they gather.

Even as Rachel cried out for her children, we **cry out for our children,** for the blood has indeed come up to the windows, and the blood of the innocent runs in the street.

We bind up **violence, anger, rage, and terror,** and it shall not come near them.

Your blood is a **wall** between them and the **rapist, drug dealer, gangs, terrorists, cults, and false religions.**

God, you preserve them from the road of destruction.

You have set before them **life and death, and they choose life.**

They will love you with all their might, heart, and mind.

They shall be **God-chasers, pursuers of your heart.**

They hear your voice, and **another they will not follow.**

They love your law and delight in it.

They seek to **please you.**

They are a **generation that shall rise up and declare your goodness.**

They shall be **greatly used by you.**

We pray for our children who live in chaotic situations, that you will **protect them** and keep them safe from hurt and harm.

We pray for those who are being raised by **grandparents or other relatives** because their parents are caught up in drugs or in prison.

We **bind up the spirits of rejection, anger, hatred, and bitterness.**

Your Word declares:

> **Romans 8:28**: "And we know that all things work together for good to them that love God, to them who are the called according to his purpose."

Work out your will in their lives.

We pray for those who have lost parents due to **tragedy or death,** that they will experience your **love and care.**

For your Word declares:

> **Psalm 68:5**: "A father of the fatherless, and a judge of the widows, is God in his holy habitation."

We decree and declare **victory in their lives.**

They have **favor in school, with peers, and with teachers.**

They are **the best of the best.**

You open up their abilities to **soak up knowledge like a sponge.**

Creativity is birthed in them.

They are entrepreneurs, designers, inventors, teachers, lawyers, doctors, and financial masters.

They are **sensitive, kind, compassionate, and giving.**

They are the **head and not the tail.**

They excel in everything they put their hands to do.

They shall not forget you but **remember you in their youth.**

They shall remember that **it is you who has given them favor, gifts, and talents to get wealth, and they shall always give you the glory.**

Every talent and gift you give them shall be used for your glory.

Bind their feet to the **path of righteousness,**

Clothe them in **sanctification,**

Perfume them with **holiness.**

Saturate them in **your love.**

Enlighten their eyes and **open up their understanding.**

We draw the **bloodline around them, under them, through them,** and make a **bold declaration** that:

Satan will not have them.

We will **never give up on them.**

We will **never let them go.**

They **belong to you,** and we commit them into your hands.

We ask that you send **warring angels** to walk with them, **ministering angels** to be with them, and that you **be a fence all around them.**

We give you **praise in advance** for how you are **keeping them, loving them, and protecting them.**

They shall be **mightily used by you.**

***

Scriptures for Meditation

• **John 1:1**: "In the beginning was the Word, and the Word was with God, and the Word was God."

- **Exodus 12:13**: "And the blood shall be to you for a token upon the houses where ye are: and when I see the blood, I will pass over you."

- **Ecclesiastes 12:1**: "Remember now thy Creator in the days of thy youth."

- **Hosea 10:12**: "Sow to yourselves in righteousness, reap in mercy."

- **Ephesians 6:1–4**: "Children, obey your parents in the Lord."

- **Isaiah 54:13**: "And all thy children shall be taught of the Lord."

- **Deuteronomy 30:15–20**: "I have set before thee life and good, and death and evil."

- **Deuteronomy 28:13**: "The Lord shall make thee the head, and not the tail."

- **Proverbs 2:20**: "That thou mayest walk in the way of good men."

- **1 Timothy 4:14–15**: "Neglect not the gift that is in thee."

- **Ephesians 1:18**: "The eyes of your understanding being enlightened."

- **2 Timothy 1:12**: "For I know whom I have believed."

- **Hebrews 1:14**: "Are they not all ministering spirits?"

- **Psalm 91:11–12**: "For he shall give his angels charge over thee."

Prayers For A Mate (Male)

SPEAK THE ANSWER, NOT THE PROBLEM.

THE ANSWER IS THE WORD OF GOD.

God, you are your Word.

You declared in your Word that **it is not good for man to be alone.** You took a rib from a man and created a woman to walk alongside him as his **helpmate.**

Heavenly Father, I am seeking that helpmate.

Please prepare me to **become a husband.**

Give me the right mindset to be a **spiritual and natural covering** for her.

Help me prepare to step into this role by securing the means to **provide for her.**

Prepare me now to **share my life with her** and to **forsake all others.**

Lead and guide me in this search so that I will be careful not to **leave a trail of broken hearts** behind on this journey.

Let me find that **precious jewel** you have for me, and I promise to **love her even as you love your church.**

Father, your Word declares:

> **Psalm 37:4**: "Delight thyself also in the Lord: and he shall give thee the desires of thine heart."

You know exactly **who I need.**

She must love you with **all her heart, mind, body, and soul,** and in this way, we will be **compatible.**

The wife for me will be:

- **Kind-hearted, compassionate, and loving**
- **Able to understand my humor** and have a sense of humor herself
- **A good housekeeper,** knowing how to build her home
- **Wise** and able to make **wise decisions**
- **A virtuous woman**

I thank you, God, that I will know **with certainty** who she is when I meet her, and you will **bless our union.**

I pray for **wisdom** to know, understand, and perceive when our paths cross that **this is indeed your will for me.**

***

Scriptures for Meditation

• **John 1:1**: "In the beginning was the Word, and the Word was with God, and the Word was God."

• **John 14:13**: "And whatsoever ye shall ask in my name, that will I do, that the Father may be glorified in the Son."

• **Genesis 2:18**: "And the Lord God said, It is not good that the man should be alone; I will make him an help meet for him."

• **Proverbs 18:22**: "Whoso findeth a wife findeth a good thing, and obtaineth favour of the Lord."

• **Proverbs 31**: A guide for the characteristics of a virtuous woman.

Prayers For A Mate (For Women)

SPEAK THE ANSWER, NOT THE PROBLEM.

THE ANSWER IS THE WORD OF GOD.

God, you are your Word.

Heavenly Father, your Word declares:

> **Psalm 37:4**: "Delight thyself also in the Lord: and he shall give thee the desires of thine heart."

I **desire to marry.**

You took the rib from a man and **created the female** to walk alongside him.

I need the man to **search and find me.**

You know **where I belong** and my need to be **placed in the right spot.**

Prepare me to be **the wife I need to be.**

Grant me wisdom now to be a **good wife and homemaker, full of wisdom.**

Teach me to be **loving, kind, compassionate, and understanding.**

Teach me now how to **prepare a budget, prepare meals, and be efficient in everything you give my hands to do.**

Let me be **the answer to his prayer.**

Prepare me to **undergird him in prayer** and to encourage him to be **the best of the best.**

I pray for **a man** who:

• **Loves you** with all his **heart, mind, body, and soul.**

• Will be a **good covering** to me and to our children.

• Will be **patient** with me and love me **in spite of my imperfections.**

• Is **resourceful and skillful.**

• Will be a **good provider** and **priest over our home.**

***

Scriptures for Meditation

• **John 1:1**: "In the beginning was the Word, and the Word was with God, and the Word was God."

• **John 14:13**: "And whatsoever ye shall ask in my name, that will I do, that the Father may be glorified in the Son."

• **Genesis 2:18**: "And the Lord God said, It is not good that the man should be alone; I will make him an help meet for him."

• **Proverbs 18:22**: "Whoso findeth a wife findeth a good thing, and obtaineth favour of the Lord."

• **Proverbs 31**: A guide for the characteristics of a virtuous woman.

• **Titus 2:3–5**: Instructions for women to be wise, kind, and keepers of the home.

• **Ephesians 5:33**: "Nevertheless let every one of you in particular so love his wife even as himself; and the wife see that she reverence her husband."

To Have Children

SPEAK THE ANSWER, NOT THE PROBLEM.

THE ANSWER IS THE WORD OF GOD.

God, you are your Word.

Heavenly Father, we stand in the gap with those families who **desire children.**

Your Word declares:

> **Psalm 37:4**: "Delight thyself also in the Lord: and he shall give thee the desires of thine heart."

Children are a blessing, and we desire this blessing.

We **lay claim to your promises** and believe that just as you **heard the prayer of Hannah** and granted her the desires of her heart, **so you will do for us as well.**

Just as you **remembered Sarah** and caused her to bear fruit in her old age, **so shall you do it for us.**

You will allow me to be a **joyful mother of children.**

I shall **not miscarry or be barren.**

Father, I know that there is some woman **who is thinking about abortion.**

I pray that you would **prevent her from doing so** and allow her to release that child for adoption.

If it is your choice for **my motherhood—our parenthood—to come through adoption, let it be so.**

We **thank you** for granting our petitions, and we give you **praise, glory, and honor** in the **precious name of your Son, Jesus Christ.**

***

Scriptures for Meditation

• **John 1:1**: "In the beginning was the Word, and the Word was with God, and the Word was God."

• **1 John 5:14–15**: "And this is the confidence that we have in him, that, if we ask any thing according to his will, he heareth us: and if we know that he hear us, whatsoever we ask, we know that we have the petitions that we desired of him."

• **Matthew 18:19–20**: "Again I say unto you, That if two of you shall agree on earth as touching any thing that they shall ask, it shall be done for them of my Father which is in heaven. For where two or three are gathered together in my name, there am I in the midst of them."

• **1 Samuel 1**: The story of Hannah's prayer and God's faithfulness in granting her a son.

• **Psalm 127:3**: "Lo, children are an heritage of the Lord: and the fruit of the womb is his reward."

• **Psalm 84:11**: "For the Lord God is a sun and shield: the Lord will give grace and glory: no good thing will he withhold from them that walk uprightly."

• **Psalm 113:9**: "He maketh the barren woman to keep house, and to be a joyful mother of children. Praise ye the Lord."

Salvation For All

SPEAK THE ANSWER, NOT THE PROBLEM.

THE ANSWER IS THE WORD OF GOD.

God, You Are Your Word, and You Watch Over It to Perform It.

So, **Heavenly Father,** your Word declares:

> **John 3:16**: "For God so loved the world, that he gave his only begotten Son, that whosoever believeth in him should not perish, but have everlasting life."

You didn't just **love us**—you **so love us.**

You love us **immensely, immeasurably, without limits.**

Your Word tells us:

> **Ezekiel 18:20**: "The soul that sinneth, it shall die."

Today, we **lift up every unsaved person** connected to us—even those we may not know are connected.

We **lift up every soul** and every **backslidden person** who is on the path of destruction.

We come as **intercessors** to stand **between them and damnation.**

We come with **the sword dipped in your blood** and declare that you are even now **cutting them free** from the hand of the enemy.

We **apply your blood** over:

• **Mind-controlling spirits**

• **Delusions**

• **Everything that stands in the way of their salvation**

The enemy has **blinded their eyes and minds** so that they cannot comprehend your **great love for them.**

Today, we declare, **through the authority of your Word** and the **power of your shed blood,** that:

> **Mind-controlling spirits**—brought on through the **open door of sin, mental illness, drugs, and delusions**—are being **not just broken but destroyed** in the name of Jesus.

We **speak to you** and say:

> *Do not believe the lie that God does not love you.*
>
> *Do not believe that you are not worthy of salvation.*

We **break off spirits of confusion and perversion.**

On your behalf, **we are walking through the valley of death** to:

• **Dig you up**

• **Pull you out**

• **Set you free**

In the name of Jesus.

We decree and declare:

• **When you call on the name of Jesus, he will come and rescue you, set you free, and deliver you.**

• **No devil in hell can hold you hostage.**

• **When you call on the name of Jesus, Jesus will send in the SWAT team.**

We decree and declare today:

• **Your eyes shall be opened.**

• **Your ears shall be opened.**

You will hear the voice of Jesus calling your name:

Come out! Come out!

From the **east, west, north, and south,** step into **the freedom of salvation.**

We send this **prayer to burn in your belly, down in your soul,** until you give God a **yes.**

We have:

• **Prayed too long**

• **Cried too long**

• **Wept, mourned, and travailed** for your soul.

And **God himself will answer our prayers.**

***

Scriptures for Meditation

• **Isaiah 65:24**: "And it shall come to pass, that before they call, I will answer; and while they are yet speaking, I will hear."

• **Jeremiah 1:12**: "Then said the Lord unto me, Thou hast well seen: for I will hasten my word to perform it."

• **John 3:16**: "For God so loved the world, that he gave his only begotten Son."

• **Ezekiel 18:20**: "The soul that sinneth, it shall die."

• **Ezekiel 22:30**: "And I sought for a man among them, that should make up the hedge, and stand in the gap before me for the land."

• **Exodus 12:13**: "And the blood shall be to you for a token upon the houses where ye are: and when I see the blood, I will pass over you."

• **Luke 10:19**: "Behold, I give unto you power to tread on serpents and scorpions, and over all the power of the enemy."

• **Mark 5:1−5**: The story of the man possessed by demons and his deliverance.

• **Ephesians 6:12**: "For we wrestle not against flesh and blood, but against principalities, against powers, against the rulers of the darkness of this world."

• **John 12:40**: "He hath blinded their eyes, and hardened their heart; that they should not see with their eyes, nor understand with their heart, and be converted, and I should heal them."

• **Job 22:28–29**: "Thou shalt also decree a thing, and it shall be established unto thee: and the light shall shine upon thy ways."

• **Psalm 23:4**: "Yea, though I walk through the valley of the shadow of death, I will fear no evil."

• **Romans 10:13**: "For whosoever shall call upon the name of the Lord shall be saved."

• **Isaiah 43:6**: "I will say to the north, Give up; and to the south, Keep not back: bring my sons from far, and my daughters from the ends of the earth."

• **Matthew 2:18**: "In Rama was there a voice heard, lamentation, and weeping, and great mourning."

• **Isaiah 30:19**: "For the people shall dwell in Zion at Jerusalem: thou shalt weep no more."

Household Salvation

SPEAK THE ANSWER, NOT THE PROBLEM.

THE ANSWER IS THE WORD OF GOD. YOU ARE YOUR WORD.

Heavenly Father, I stand in the gap for every family member **for their salvation.**

Your Word declares:

> **Acts 16:31**: "Believe on the Lord Jesus Christ, and thou shalt be saved, and thy house."

I bind up **every opposing demonic force** that tries to keep them in **bondage.**

I **loose them** from the power of darkness and call them to walk in the **marvelous light** of your salvation.

I decree that:

• **Blinded eyes** are being opened to see your **nail-scarred hands** reaching out to them.

• **Stopped-up ears** are opened to hear **your voice** calling them to salvation.

Thank you, God, for:

• Giving them **a heart transplant** and circumcising their hearts to be tender toward you.

• Destroying **every argument** that Satan presents to them in the **name of Jesus.**

• Giving them **a mind transplant** and causing their minds to be **renewed in righteousness.**

We (myself and every believer) **walk through the valley of the shadow of death** to **pull them out of the graveyard of sin.**

We say to the **north, give them up; to the south, keep not back.**

Let the **winds blow from the four corners of the earth** and blow them into **the ark of safety.**

Let your **Holy Spirit** be as a **mighty broom** and **sweep them** into the place of **repentance.**

Let them **call upon your name** and seek you **with their whole heart.**

Destroy every ungodly soul tie.

Wash them in the blood of your Son, Jesus.

Clean them through the power of your Holy Word and set them free.

Send ministering angels to minister to them and bind up every **hurt and disappointment** of the past.

Send your warring angels to war on their behalf **until they become rooted and grounded in your Word.**

Fill them with your **Holy Spirit** to lead and guide them into **all truth.**

Let **all of heaven rejoice** at their salvation.

Pour out your Spirit on them, and let them **dream dreams and see visions.**

I decree and declare:

• They will **love you** with all their **heart, mind, body, soul, and spirit.**

• You will make them **mighty weapons of war in your hands.**

For this cause, we **bow our knees, lift up our voices, and worship you, God,** for **you alone are worthy of the praise.**

***

Scriptures for Meditation

• **Exodus 22:30–31**: " Likewise shalt thou do with thine oxen, and with thy sheep: seven days it shall be with his dam; on the eighth day thou shalt give it me. And ye shall be holy men unto me: neither shall ye eat any flesh that is torn of beasts in the field; ye shall cast it to the dogs."

• **Acts 16:31**: "And they said, Believe on the Lord Jesus Christ, and thou shalt be saved, and thy house."

• **Matthew 18:18–20**: "Verily I say unto you, Whatsoever ye shall bind on earth shall be bound in heaven: and whatsoever ye shall loose on earth shall be loosed in heaven. Again I say unto you, That if two of you shall agree on earth as touching any thing that they shall ask, it shall be done for them of my Father which is in heaven. For where two or three are gathered together in my name, there am I in the midst of them."

- **1 Peter 2:9**: " But ye are a chosen generation, a royal priesthood, an holy nation, a peculiar people; that ye should shew forth the praises of him who hath called you out of darkness into his marvellous light."

- **Psalm 23:4**: " Yea, though I walk through the valley of the shadow of death, I will fear no evil: for thou art with me; thy rod and thy staff they comfort me."

- **Romans 10:13**: " For whosoever shall call upon the name of the Lord shall be saved."

- **Isaiah 42:7**: "To open the blind eyes, to bring out the prisoners from the prison, and them that sit in darkness out of the prison house."

- **Isaiah 35:5**: "Then the eyes of the blind shall be opened, and the ears of the deaf shall be unstopped."

- **Ezekiel 36:26**: "A new heart also will I give you, and a new spirit will I put within you: and I will take away the stony heart out of your flesh, and I will give you an heart of flesh."

- **2 Corinthians 10:5–8:** "Casting down imaginations, and every high thing that exalteth itself against the knowledge of God, and bringing into captivity every thought to the obedience of Christ. And having in a readiness to revenge all disobedience, when your obedience is fulfilled. Do ye look on things after the outward appearance? If any man trust to himself that he is Christ's, let him of himself think this again, that, as he is Christ's, even so are we Christ's. For though I should boast somewhat more of our authority, which the Lord hath given us for edification, and not for your destruction, I should not be ashamed."

• **Romans 12:2**: "And be not conformed to this world: but be ye transformed by the renewing of your mind, that ye may prove what is that good, and acceptable, and perfect, will of God."

• **Isaiah 43:6:** " I will say to the north, Give up; and to the south, Keep not back: bring my sons from far, and my daughters from the ends of the earth."

• **1 John 1:7**: " But if we walk in the light, as he is in the light, we have fellowship one with another, and the blood of Jesus Christ his Son cleanseth us from all sin."

• **Ephesians 1:7**: " In whom we have redemption through his blood, the forgiveness of sins, according to the riches of his grace."

• **Hebrews 1:14**: "Are they not all ministering spirits, sent forth to minister for them who shall be heirs of salvation?"

• **Daniel 10:13–21**: "But the prince of the kingdom of Persia withstood me one and twenty days: but, lo, Michael, one of the chief princes, came to help me; and I remained there with the kings of Persia. Now I am come to make thee understand what shall befall thy people in the latter days: for yet the vision is for many days. And when he had spoken such words unto me, I set my face toward the ground, and I became dumb. And, behold, one like the similitude of the sons of men touched my lips: then I opened my mouth, and spake, and said unto him that stood before me, O my lord, by the vision my sorrows are turned upon me, and I have retained no strength. For how can the servant of this my lord talk with this my lord? for as for me, straightway there remained no strength in me, neither is there breath left in me. Then there came again and touched me one like the appearance of a man, and he strengthened me, And said, O man greatly beloved, fear not: peace be unto thee, be strong, yea, be strong. And when he had spoken unto me, I was strengthened, and said, Let my lord speak; for thou hast strengthened me. Then said he, Knowest thou wherefore I come unto thee? and now will I return to fight with the prince of Persia: and when I am gone forth, lo, the prince of Grecia shall come. But I will shew thee that which is noted in the scripture of truth: and there is none that holdeth with me in these things, but Michael your prince."

• **John 16:13**: "Howbeit when he, the Spirit of truth, is come, he will guide you into all truth: for he shall not speak of himself; but whatsoever he shall hear, that shall he speak: and he will shew you things to come."

• **Luke 15:7–10**: "I say unto you, that likewise joy shall be in heaven over one sinner that repenteth, more than over ninety and nine just persons, which need no repentance. Either what woman having ten pieces of silver, if she lose one piece, doth not light a candle, and sweep the house, and seek diligently till she find it? And when she hath found it, she calleth her friends and her neighbours together, saying, Rejoice with me; for I have found the piece which I had lost. Likewise, I say unto you, there is joy in the presence of the angels of God over one sinner that repenteth."

• **Acts 2:17**: " And it shall come to pass in the last days, saith God, I will pour out of my Spirit upon all flesh: and your sons and your daughters shall prophesy, and your young men shall see visions, and your old men shall dream dreams."

• **Matthew 22:37**: "Jesus said unto him, Thou shalt love the Lord thy God with all thy heart, and with all thy soul, and with all thy mind."

• **Ephesians 3:14**: "For this cause I bow my knees unto the Father of our Lord Jesus Christ."

• **Psalm 95:6–7**: "O come, let us worship and bow down: let us kneel before the Lord our maker. For he is our God; and we are the people of his pasture, and the sheep of his hand. To day if ye will hear his voice."

Note: This is how you bathe your prayers in the word. God is his word and his word never fails.

Prayers For Our Pastors

SPEAK THE ANSWER, NOT THE PROBLEM.

YOUR WORD IS THE ANSWER, AND YOU ARE YOUR WORD.

Heavenly Father, today as we come to you, we pray for our **priests, pastors, leaders, and shepherds.**

We **lift up each and every one of them,** and we decree according to your Word that **you give us pastors after your own heart.**

We pray that the **spirit of conviction and repentance** falls upon every pastor.

We call them **back to the altar** and ask that you release:
• **A weeping spirit upon them.**
• **A burden for the lost, the hurting, the brokenhearted, the sick, and the lost everywhere.**

We decree and declare that they shall:

• **Cry aloud and spare not.**

• **Proclaim a solemn fast** for your people and **lead the way back to the old landmark.**

• **Speak boldly** the truth and **not be ashamed** or afraid of the people's faces.

• **Declare your Word** without fear of what others will say or think.

We decree and declare that:

• **Wisdom, knowledge, skill, and understanding** are theirs.

• **The fivefold ministry** operates in their lives.

• They are **clothed in sanctification** and **perfumed with holiness.**

• You anoint their heads with the **fresh liquid oil** of your anointing.

• They seek you **with all their heart, mind, body, and soul.**

• They are **100% committed** to bringing glory to your name.

They are a **gift to the body of Christ** and take care of the **temple you have given them** by being mindful of their:

• **Health issues**

• **Sleep and rest**

• **Personal family responsibilities**

You keep them **free from sin and shame.**

You appoint **intercessors** to **stand in the gap for them.**

We ask you to send:

• **Warring angels** to assist them in the warfare that will come as they recommit to you.

• **Ministering angels** to meet their every need.

We **cover them**—their ministries, homes, families, finances, and every aspect of their lives—with your **blood.**

We decree and declare that they are the **priests of their homes** and they guide their families with **love and compassion.**

They are:

• **Tenderhearted toward their loved ones** and give them **individual attention.**

• **Not too busy to hear the hearts of their own family members.**

• **Making time for family vacations and togetherness.**

• **Not engaging in verbal or physical domestic violence.**

They are **good stewards** over their **personal family finances.**

Now, Father, we **bow down before you** and thank you for:

• **A refreshing, reviving, and restoration** of the priest and ministers of the Lord.

• **A renewal of their commitment** to serve your people in righteousness.

We **worship you and give you glory** because you are **that you are**—

• **Almighty**

• **All-powerful**

• **The God who rules, abides, and reigns**

***

Scriptures for Meditation

• **Jeremiah 3:15**: "And I will give you pastors according to mine heart, which shall feed you with knowledge and understanding."

• **Joel 2:17**: "Let the priests, the ministers of the Lord, weep between the porch and the altar, and let them say, Spare thy people, O Lord, and give not thine heritage to reproach, that the heathen should rule over them: wherefore should they say among the people, Where is their God?"

• **Luke 4:18**: "The Spirit of the Lord is upon me, because he hath anointed me to preach the gospel to the poor; he hath sent me to heal the broken-hearted, to preach deliverance to the captives, and recovering of sight to the blind, to set at liberty them that are bruised."

• **1 Timothy 3:1–2**: "This is a true saying, If a man desire the office of a bishop, he desireth a good work. A bishop then must be blameless, the husband of one wife, vigilant, sober, of good behaviour, given to hospitality, apt to teach."

• **Isaiah 58:1–2**: "Cry aloud, spare not, lift up thy voice like a trumpet, and shew my people their transgression, and the house of Jacob their sins. Yet they seek me daily, and delight to know my ways, as a nation that did righteousness, and forsook not the ordinance of their God: they ask of me the ordinances of justice; they take delight in approaching to God."

• **Isaiah 11:2**: "And the spirit of the Lord shall rest upon him, the spirit of wisdom and understanding, the spirit of counsel and might, the spirit of knowledge and of the fear of the Lord."

• **Psalm 133:2**: "It is like the precious ointment upon the head, that ran down upon the beard, even Aaron's beard: that went down to the skirts of his garments."

• **Joel 1:14**: "Sanctify ye a fast, call a solemn assembly, gather the elders and all the inhabitants of the land into the house of the Lord your God, and cry unto the Lord."

• **1 Thessalonians 4:4**: "That every one of you should know how to possess his vessel in sanctification and honour."

• **2 Corinthians 2:15**: "For we are unto God a sweet savour of Christ, in them that are saved, and in them that perish."

• **1 Timothy 5:8**: "But if any provide not for his own, and specially for those of his own house, he hath denied the faith, and is worse than an infidel."

• **1 Peter 3:7**: "Likewise, ye husbands, dwell with them according to knowledge, giving honour unto the wife, as unto the weaker vessel, and as being heirs together of the grace of life; that your prayers be not hindered."

So many more scriptures are incorporated in this prayer. You identify them.

Prayers For The Lady of the Church

Marriage is **hard work** for any person. Marriage for those in **ministry** is even more difficult.

The **First Lady** or **Lady of the Church** faces **unique challenges**—even down to the basic question of **how she should be addressed.**

• **First Lady**

• **Lady of the Church**

• **Co-pastor**

Many **struggle** with questions such as:

• *What is my role in the ministry?*

• *Who am I?*

• *Am I valuable?*

• *Am I needed?*

• *What is my purpose?*

***

SPEAK THE ANSWER, NOT THE PROBLEM.

YOUR WORD IS THE ANSWER, AND YOU ARE YOUR WORD.

God, you are your Word.

We **stand in the gap** for the **First Lady of the Church.**

She **exemplifies Proverbs 31.**

She **raises the bar** for other women to see and **challenges them** to walk according to **your Word.**

She **walks in humility** and possesses **amazing strength and grace.**

She is **down-to-earth** and not **full of pride.**

She is **confident** in who she is and **who she is in you.**

You give her **wisdom** in how to **come in and go out among the people.**

She is able to **withstand the scrutiny of others,** and her **peace is undisturbed.**

She is blessed with:

• The **spirit of wisdom and understanding**

• The **spirit of counsel and might**

• The **spirit of knowledge and the fear of the Lord**

These **rest upon her.**

Her **beauty comes from within,** and she is **not conceited.**

She **conquers her enemy** by her **steadfast love** for you.

Others **see her** and know, above all, that **she is a woman of God.**

She has **discernment** and sees the enemy **from afar off.**

She knows how to **prepare** for the **attack of the enemy.**

She **fiercely guards** her **home, family, and marriage** from the onslaught of the enemy.

Her love is like **the mustard seed**—small at first, but **growing large enough for the birds to nest in its branches.**

She is a **prayer warrior and a worshipper,** seeking the **face of God often.**

She is the **greatest intercessor** her husband will ever have.

She knows how to **undergird him and the ministry** they share.

She is **watchful over their children** and guards them from **the on-slaught of criticism** from others.

She **hears the voice of God** and walks **obediently** in response.

She has **a ministry within her** and actively **pursues the vision** God has given her.

She **walks in her purpose.**

***

Scriptures for Meditation

• **Proverbs 31**: The virtues of a godly woman

• **1 Peter 5:5**: "Likewise, ye younger, submit yourselves unto the elder. Yea, all of you be subject one to another, and be clothed with humility: for God resisteth the proud, and giveth grace to the humble."

• **Psalm 149:4**: "For the Lord taketh pleasure in his people: he will beautify the meek with salvation."

• **Romans 8:15**: "For ye have not received the spirit of bondage again to fear; but ye have received the Spirit of adoption, whereby we cry, Abba, Father."

• **Isaiah 11:2**: "And the spirit of the Lord shall rest upon him, the spirit of wisdom and understanding, the spirit of counsel and might, the spirit of knowledge and of the fear of the Lord."

• **1 Samuel 3:7–10**: The call of Samuel and his response to God's voice

Husband of the Pastor

Co-Pastor, First Man, First Gentlemen. These are **titles** that may be given to the **husband of the Pastor/Wife.**

He is the **man of the house** and the **priest of the home**, yet his wife is the **Pastor.**

He faces **unique challenges** in this position.

***

SPEAK THE ANSWER, NOT THE PROBLEM.

YOUR WORD IS THE ANSWER, AND YOU ARE YOUR WORD.

God, your Word is the answer.

You are your Word.

You created **man** to be the **head of the household.**

You created him to be the **priest of his home.**

I make the following **decrees** over his life:

• **You are a strong, godly man, fully equipped to handle the challenges of this position.**

• **You know who you are in God and are not intimidated by the opinions of others.**

• **You seamlessly balance your roles as the priest of your home and as the husband of a pastor.**

• **Your wife understands her role as Pastor and seamlessly transitions between being a pastor and a submissive wife in the home.**

• **You are not intimidated when your wife functions as the pastor, addressing the concerns of both men and women in the flock.**

• **You have God-given wisdom on how to protect her without operating out of jealousy.**

• **You carry out your role as the priest of the home royally and without resentment, bitterness, or fear.**

• **You allow the Holy Spirit to guide you in operating within your role.**

Not every man can handle the role of having a wife who is a pastor without feeling a loss of his manhood—but you, sir, are built for this role.

• As the priest, you establish the rules and expectations for your home.

• As a servant of God, you give your wife the support and freedom to be who God has called her to be.

• As the priest, you cover her in prayer.

• As a servant, you are her strongest intercessor.

• As the pastor, she walks in her authority.

• As the priest of the house, you rule with loving-kindness.

• As pastor, priest, husband, and wife, you move as one complete body—walking in unity and harmony.

True Prophets

SPEAK THE ANSWER, NOT THE PROBLEM.

The Answer Is the Word of God.

God, you are your Word.

We **stand in the gap** for the **prophets.**

Your Word speaks of **false prophets and true prophets.**

We **decree and declare** that:

• **The fear of God will fall upon every false prophet, leading them to repentance before they are exposed.**

• **The true prophets are those whom you have called to proclaim the truth of your Word.**

• **They move in integrity and truth, foretelling only that which you give them.**

• **They warn, rebuke, and call your people to repentance.**

Thank you, God, for the **true prophets** whom you **knew and ordained** before they ever entered this world.

You have **touched their lips** with the **hot coals of fire** that **purify them.**

You have **put your words in their mouths.**

They **walk close to you** so they may hear the words that you speak.

They **dare not speak** what you have not released them to speak, for those who do so will surely die.

They **do not speak** their own thoughts or desires—

Only what **you give them to declare.**

They **do not refuse** to speak what you have commanded them to release.

The word of a **true prophet** will **not fall to the ground.**

You give them **courage and holy boldness** to **declare truth**—

Even when **many may not want to hear or receive it.**

You make **yourself known to them.**

There is **nothing you do in the earth realm** without revealing it to your **true prophets.**

They are **transformed by your Word** and able to **discern truth.**

They **seek your face, hear your voice, and obey your commands.**

You cause the **words they speak to manifest,** so the people will know that they are indeed your **true prophets.**

Father, thank you for keeping them **safe** from the **backlash of the enemy.**

You give them:

• **Physical strength**

• **Emotional strength**

• **Spiritual strength**

To carry out **their assignments.**

Your **blood covers** their:

• **Mind**

• **Spirit**

• **Physical body**

From the **attacks of the enemy.**

You assign **ministering and warring angels** to:

• **Guard them**

• **Comfort them**

You **order their footsteps,** and your Word is **fire in their belly.**

***

Scriptures for Meditation

• **Deuteronomy 18:20**: "But the prophet, which shall presume to speak a word in my name, which I have not commanded him to speak, or that shall speak in the name of other gods, even that prophet shall die."

• **Amos 3:7**: "Surely the Lord God will do nothing, but he revealeth his secret unto his servants the prophets."

• **Jeremiah 1:9**: "Then the Lord put forth his hand, and touched my mouth. And the Lord said unto me, Behold, I have put my words in thy mouth."

• **Psalm 139:13–18**: "For thou hast possessed my reins: thou hast covered me in my mother's womb."

• **Isaiah 6:6–7**: "Then flew one of the seraphims unto me, having a live coal in his hand, which he had taken with the tongs from off the altar: And he laid it upon my mouth, and said, Lo, this hath touched thy lips; and thine iniquity is taken away, and thy sin purged."

• **Isaiah 55:10–11**: "So shall my word be that goeth forth out of my mouth: it shall not return unto me void, but it shall accomplish that which I please, and it shall prosper in the thing whereto I sent it."

• **Jeremiah 20:9**: "But his word was in mine heart as a burning fire shut up in my bones, and I was weary with forbearing, and I could not stay."

• **Isaiah 54:17**: "No weapon that is formed against thee shall prosper; and every tongue that shall rise against thee in judgment thou shalt condemn."

Prayers For Youth

SPEAK THE ANSWER, NOT THE PROBLEM.

The Answer Is the Word of God.

Father God, I plead the **blood of Jesus** over our youth.

Father, we pray that our youth will **acknowledge you as their Savior** while they are young.

We pray that they will have a **hunger and thirst** to know you in an **intimate way.**

Open their eyes and let them see **your goodness.**

Open their ears and let them hear **your voice.**

Transform their minds and let them seek **you wholeheartedly.**

We pray that they:

• **Surrender their bodies, minds, and spirits** to you and are **completely yielded** to your will.

• **Love you with all their might, strength, heart, and mind.**

• **See you revealed** in a way they can **understand.**

• **Are appointed mentors** who will guide, direct, and inspire them to do what is **right in your sight.**

• **Are drawn to those** who exemplify **good character and righteous living.**

• **Are drawn to the place of worship.**

Put your **Spirit within them** and let them seek to be **transformed by your Word.**

We **decree** that you are raising up a **new generation** of:

• **David**—bold and after your heart

• **Daniel**—steadfast in faith

• **Jeremiah**—called to speak your Word

• **Joseph**—wise and favored

• **Esther**—brave and purpose-driven

• **Shadrach, Meshach, and Abednego**—uncompromising in righteousness

• **Timothy**—faithful in youth and calling

• **Mary**—humble and obedient

• **Moses**—a leader and deliverer

We **call them forth** to be as the **young boy** who brought his lunch to Jesus, willingly sharing what he had.

Just as **Jesus took what was given, blessed it, and multiplied it** to feed the multitudes, let our youth **share the Word of God with others.**

Let them be as:

• **Miriam**, who watched over her brother and saw Pharaoh's daughter take him in.

• **Miriam**, who had the wisdom of God to suggest her own mother as his caretaker.

Let them have **the wisdom of God.**

Let them be as:

• **Jeremiah**, who boldly opened his mouth to declare **the Word of God.**

• **Timothy**, who did not despise his youth but embraced the **gifts placed within him.**

• **Samuel**, who **learned to hear and respond** to your voice.

• **Jesus**, who **grew in wisdom and stature, and in favor with God and man.**

***

Scriptures for Meditation

• **Ecclesiastes 12:1**: "Remember now thy Creator in the days of thy youth, while the evil days come not."

• **Matthew 5:6**: "Blessed are they which do hunger and thirst after righteousness: for they shall be filled."

• **Jeremiah 31:3**: "The Lord hath appeared of old unto me, saying, Yea, I have loved thee with an everlasting love."

• **Proverbs 4:20**: "My son, attend to my words; incline thine ear unto my sayings."

• **Romans 12:2**: "Be not conformed to this world: but be ye transformed by the renewing of your mind."

• **Luke 2:52**: "And Jesus increased in wisdom and stature, and in favour with God and man."

WISDOM AS A COUNSELOR

SPEAK THE ANSWER, NOT THE PROBLEM.

Your Word is the answer, and you are your Word.

Heavenly Father, I ask you for **divine wisdom from heaven** so that I may know how to answer the person standing in need of **guidance.**

Your Word **gives me permission** to ask you for that wisdom.

I acknowledge that **wisdom comes from you** and not just from my own ability.

Help me to **use every tool** available to me to help others.

I **look to you** to direct my path and order my steps, so that the words I speak **bring comfort to the hearer.**

Help me **not to be quick** to offer solutions but to gently **guide** the person to the truth **that already lies within them.**

Assist me in helping them **examine their needs and motives.**

Teach me how to be **supportive yet courageous** enough to **redirect them** when they are off course.

God, put your words in my mouth and let me speak them with:

• **Boldness**

• **Compassion**

• **Truth**

Let my words cause them to:

• **Examine their issues**

• **Face their challenges head-on**

Let my advice be **Christ-centered** and **seasoned with grace.**

Let the **ears of their inner man be enlightened** as I speak the words you give me to speak.

Help me to **see what is not obvious.**

Help me to **hear with my heart.**

Help me **not to be judgmental** in actions or deeds.

Help me to show **compassion and empathy** for each individual I encounter.

***

Scriptures for Meditation

• **1 John 1:1**: "That which was from the beginning, which we have heard, which we have seen with our eyes, which we have looked upon, and our hands have handled, of the Word of life."

• **James 5:12**: "But above all things, my brethren, swear not, neither by heaven, neither by the earth, neither by any other oath: but let your yea be yea; and your nay, nay; lest ye fall into condemnation."

• **Hebrews 4:16**: "Let us therefore come boldly unto the throne of grace, that we may obtain mercy, and find grace to help in time of need."

• **Daniel 1:4**: "Children in whom was no blemish, but well favored, and skillful in all wisdom, and cunning in knowledge, and understanding science, and such as had ability in them to stand in the king's palace, and whom they might teach the learning and the tongue of the Chaldeans."

• **Jeremiah 1:9**: "Then the Lord put forth his hand, and touched my mouth. And the Lord said unto me, Behold, I have put my words in thy mouth."

Prayer For Directions

SPEAK THE ANSWER, NOT THE PROBLEM.

Heavenly Father, I touch and agree for **direction** in making every decision.

We come **boldly and confidently** before your throne, according to your Word:

> **1 John 5:14**: "And this is the confidence that we have in him, that, if we ask any thing according to his will, he heareth us."

I **decree and declare** that:

• The **blood of Jesus** covers every area of your life.

• **God will cause you to know the way** you should go.

• **His Word is a lamp unto your feet and a light unto your path.**

• **God orders your steps** because you put your **trust in him** and acknowledge him **in all your ways.**

• **When you delight yourself in God,** he will give you the **desires of your heart** and **perfect those things that concern you.**

We pray and agree that the **power of the Holy Spirit**—our guide from this life to the next—will:

• **Train your spiritual eyes** to wait on God.

• **Quiet your soul** before him.

• **Guide you with his eyes** and show you **his path.**

His Word instructs us to come to him and **ask for wisdom.**

The favor of God encompasses you **like a shield.**

For this cause, **we worship and bow down** before our Lord and **praise him for the victory.**

Confess this prayer daily until God **reveals his plan** to you.

Do not be anxious, but trust God as you **worship him daily.**

***

Scriptures for Meditation

• **Matthew 18:19–20**: "Again I say unto you, That if two of you shall agree on earth as touching any thing that they shall ask, it shall be done for them of my Father which is in heaven."

• **Hebrews 4:16**: "Let us therefore come boldly unto the throne of grace, that we may obtain mercy, and find grace to help in time of need."

• **1 John 5:14–15**: "And this is the confidence that we have in him, that, if we ask any thing according to his will, he heareth us."

• **Exodus 12:13**: "And the blood shall be to you for a token upon the houses where ye are: and when I see the blood, I will pass over you."

• **Psalm 25:4–6**: "Shew me thy ways, O Lord; teach me thy paths. Lead me in thy truth, and teach me: for thou art the God of my salvation."

• **Psalm 119:105**: "Thy word is a lamp unto my feet, and a light unto my path."

• **Psalm 37:23**: "The steps of a good man are ordered by the Lord: and he delighteth in his way."

• **Proverbs 3:5–7**: "Trust in the Lord with all thine heart; and lean not unto thine own understanding."

• **Psalm 37:4**: "Delight thyself also in the Lord; and he shall give thee the desires of thine heart."

• **Psalm 32:8**: "I will instruct thee and teach thee in the way which thou shalt go: I will guide thee with mine eye."

• **Isaiah 30:21**: "And thine ears shall hear a word behind thee, saying, This is the way, walk ye in it, when ye turn to the right hand, and when ye turn to the left."

• **James 1:5**: "If any of you lack wisdom, let him ask of God, that giveth to all men liberally, and upbraideth not; and it shall be given him."

• **Psalm 5:12**: "For thou, Lord, wilt bless the righteous; with favour wilt thou compass him as with a shield."

• **Psalm 95:1–6**: "O come, let us sing unto the Lord: let us make a joyful noise to the rock of our salvation."

BROKENNESS

This example addresses those whose **life experiences** have left them **broken** due to:

• **Troubled or failed relationships**

• **"Church hurt"**

In this journey called **life,** we will encounter **many tests** in these areas.

The **enemy is crafty**—he **magnifies** our **hurts and insecurities.**

Be diligent in understanding that **it was not God,** your **Heavenly Father,** who "hurt" you.

It was **Satan working through a person.**

So do not **run away from God** because of your experience.

Instead, **run to him.**

***

SPEAK THE ANSWER, NOT THE PROBLEM.

THE ANSWER IS THE WORD OF GOD

Heavenly Father, we thank you for the **power of agreement.**

There are times when we must **access that power** by finding a **trusted person** to stand in agreement with us.

When we are **not comfortable trusting someone else,** we come into **agreement with you** and stretch our hands out to you.

Thank you for the **shed blood of Jesus** and your **Holy Word** that comes to make us **whole.**

We **release your Word** of **comfort, hope, and love** over:

- **Every broken heart**
- **Every wounded spirit**
- **Every bowed-down head**

We **release your Word** over every person who feels:

- **Rejected**
- **Misunderstood**
- **Cut off**
- **Confused**
- **Frustrated**

We pray especially for those who have been **hurt in the church** and ask that you:

• **Draw them to you.**

• **Do not let them turn away** from the **only one** who has the **words of life and comfort.**

• Let them **seek you with all their heart, mind, and soul.**

• Let them **pour out their hearts to you** and never, ever **doubt your love** for them.

Let them **run into your arms** like a little child needing:

• The **warm embrace**

• The **comforting touch** of a loving Father

• The **assurance that everything will be alright**

One **word from you** changes our life.

One **touch from you** wipes away **every tear.**

For this cause, we **bow our knees** to you.

We **lift up our hands** in **total worship,** for surely **there is none like you.**

You are:

• **God**

• **All-powerful**

- **All-knowing**

- **Loving**

- **Caring**

- **Protecting**

Even in the **night season** of our lives, we say:

Thank you for loving us.

We **love you, Father.**

We **bless your holy name,** giving you **all the glory** because **you are ever worthy** of our **love and praise.**

***

Scriptures for Meditation

- **Matthew 18:19**: "Again I say unto you, That if two of you shall agree on earth as touching any thing that they shall ask, it shall be done for them of my Father which is in heaven."

- **Psalm 88:13**: "But unto thee have I cried, O Lord; and in the morning shall my prayer prevent thee."

- **Psalm 121:1**: "I will lift up mine eyes unto the hills, from whence cometh my help."

- **Leviticus 17:11**: "For the life of the flesh is in the blood: and I have given it to you upon the altar to make an atonement for your souls."

- **Psalm 3:1–8**: "Lord, how are they increased that trouble me! many are they that rise up against me."

- **Psalm 147:3**: "He healeth the broken in heart, and bindeth up their wounds."

- **Matthew 11:28–30**: "Come unto me, all ye that labour and are heavy laden, and I will give you rest."

- **Psalm 62:8**: "Trust in him at all times; ye people, pour out your heart before him: God is a refuge for us."

- **John 3:16**: "For God so loved the world, that he gave his only begotten Son, that whosoever believeth in him should not perish, but have everlasting life."

- **Isaiah 33:2**: "O Lord, be gracious unto us; we have waited for thee: be thou their arm every morning, our salvation also in the time of trouble."

• **Psalm 95:6**: "O come, let us worship and bow down: let us kneel before the Lord our maker."

• **Habakkuk 3:17–18**: "Although the fig tree shall not blossom, neither shall fruit be in the vines; the labour of the olive shall fail, and the fields shall yield no meat; the flock shall be cut off from the fold, and there shall be no herd in the stalls: Yet I will rejoice in the Lord, I will joy in the God of my salvation."

FEAR

SPEAK THE ANSWER, NOT THE PROBLEM.

Heavenly Father,

We touch and agree with _____ according to Your Word. You have not given us the spirit of fear, but of power, and of love, and of a sound mind. I believe Your Word, and it declares over and over to **not be afraid.**

• **Psalm 23:4**: "Even though I walk through the darkest valley, I will fear no evil, for you are with me; your rod and your staff, they comfort me."

• **Psalm 56:3–4**: "When I am afraid, I put my trust in you. In God, whose word I praise—in God I trust and am not afraid. What can mere mortals do to me?"

• **Proverbs 3:24**: "When you lie down, you will not be afraid; when you lie down, your sleep will be sweet."

• **Isaiah 12:2**: "Surely God is my salvation; I will trust and not be afraid. The Lord, the Lord himself, is my strength and my defense; he has become my salvation."

• **Psalm 91:5**: "You will not fear the terror of night, nor the arrow that flies by day."

• **Isaiah 41:10**: "So do not fear, for I am with you; be not dismayed, for I am your God; I will strengthen you, I will help you, I will uphold you with my righteous right hand."

• **Deuteronomy 31:6**: "Be strong and of good courage, fear not, nor be afraid of them: for the Lord thy God, he it is that doth go with thee; he will not fail thee, nor forsake thee."

• **Isaiah 43:1**: "But now thus says the Lord, he who created you, O Jacob, he who formed you, O Israel: 'Fear not, for I have redeemed you; I have called you by name; you are mine.'"

• **Hebrews 13:6**: "So we can confidently say, 'The Lord is my helper; I will not be afraid. What can mere mortals do to me?'"

God, we speak your Word, we trust your Word, and we believe your Word.

Therefore, we **serve notice** on the enemy:

Satan, the Lord rebuke you!

We stand **on the Word of God.**

Fear is not my portion.

Isolation

SPEAK THE ANSWER, NOT THE PROBLEM.

God, you are your Word.

Heavenly Father, we thank you for the **shed blood of your Son, Jesus,** and your **Holy Word** that comes to make us **whole.**

We **release your Word** of:

• **Comfort**

• **Hope**

• **Love**

Over:

• **Every broken heart**

• **Every wounded spirit**

• **Every bowed-down head**

We **send your Word** to those who feel:

• **Rejected**

- **Misunderstood**

- **Cut off**

- **Confused**

- **Frustrated**

We pray especially for those who have been **hurt in the church.**

God, draw them to you.

Do not let them **turn away** from the only **One** who has the **words of life and comfort.**

The **enemy** wants them to feel:

- **Isolated**

- **Forgotten**

- **Alone**

We **expose that lie.**

Your **Word assures us** that you are **always with us.**

You **promise never to leave us alone.**

You will **never forsake us** and you **cannot forget us.**

Let them **remember** that:

- **Your eyes see everything**—nothing is hidden from you.

- **You see them** and are concerned about **everything** that concerns them.

- **They are not isolated**—they are in a place of **incubation.**

This time of **incubation** is a time of:

- **Protection**

- **Growth**

- **Healing of heart issues**

You are using this time to:

- **Develop inner strength**

- **Teach them to trust your love**—even when they do not feel you

- **Guide them in a faith walk**—not by sight, not by emotions, but **by faith**

- **Heart**

- **Mind**

- **Soul**

Let them **pour out their hearts** to you and never, ever **doubt your love.**

Let them **run to your arms** like a little child, needing to feel:

- **Your warm embrace**

- **Your comforting touch**

You are the **loving Father** who is able to **make everything right.**

For this cause, we **bow our knees** to you.

We **lift our hands** in **total worship,** for surely **there is none like you.**

You are:

• **God**

• **All-powerful**

• **All-knowing**

• **Loving**

• **Caring**

• **Protecting**

Even in the **night seasons** of our lives, we say:

Thank you for loving us the way you do.

We **confess our love** for you.

We **bless your holy name** and give you:

• **All the glory**

• **All the praise**

• **All the honor**

Because **you are worthy of our love and praise.**

***

Scriptures for Meditation

• **John 1:1**: "In the beginning was the Word, and the Word was with God, and the Word was God."

• **Matthew 18:19–20**: "Again I say unto you, That if two of you shall agree on earth as touching any thing that they shall ask, it shall be done for them of my Father which is in heaven."

• **Exodus 12:13**: "And the blood shall be to you for a token upon the houses where ye are: and when I see the blood, I will pass over you."

• **Hebrews 4:16**: "Let us therefore come boldly unto the throne of grace, that we may obtain mercy, and find grace to help in time of need."

• **James 4:8**: "Draw nigh to God, and he will draw nigh to you."

• **Psalm 145:14**: "The Lord upholdeth all that fall, and raiseth up all those that be bowed down."

• **Deuteronomy 31:8**: "And the Lord, he it is that doth go before thee; he will be with thee, he will not fail thee, neither forsake thee: fear not, neither be dismayed."

• **Isaiah 49:15**: "Can a woman forget her sucking child, that she should not have compassion on the son of her womb? Yea, they may forget, yet will I not forget thee."

• **Genesis 16:13**: "And she called the name of the Lord that spake unto her, Thou God seest me."

• **Psalm 95:6–7**: "O come, let us worship and bow down: let us kneel before the Lord our maker. For he is our God; and we are the people of his pasture, and the sheep of his hand."

Depression

SPEAK THE ANSWER, NOT THE PROBLEM.

THE ANSWER IS THE WORD OF GOD

Heavenly Father, we come asking you to **release the blood of Jesus** over every person dealing with **depression.**

The **39 stripes** on your body **guarantee our healing—**

Healing for:
- **The body**
- **The mind**
- **The will**
- **The spirit**
- **The emotions**

We **come against the power of darkness** that brings:
- **Pain**
- **Torment**

- **Sorrow**

- **Guilt**

- **Shame**

We **receive the abundant life** that you have **ordained** for us.

We **speak to the chemicals in the brain** that they:

- **Become regulated**

- **Function as they should**

We **speak to these chemicals** in the brain:

- **Norepinephrine**

- **Serotonin**

- **Dopamine**

We **declare that the neurotransmitters** function **normally.**

The **Holy Spirit changes our appetite** and teaches us:

- **How to eat nutritious meals**

- **How to cook our food properly**

We **respond to and stand on your Word**:

"Rejoice! Again I say, rejoice!"

God gives us **a mind to worship him.**

As we **spend time in worship,** you will heal our:

• **Mind**

• **Will**

• **Emotions**

• **Spirit**

We **change our garments** and put on the **garment of praise.**

"Why are you cast down, O my soul? And why are you disquieted within me? Hope in God: for I shall yet praise him, who is the health of my countenance, and my God."

I decree and declare:
• **I will not die but live**
• **I will declare the works of God**

***

Scriptures for Meditation

• **Proverbs 18:21**: "Death and life are in the power of the tongue: and they that love it shall eat the fruit thereof."

• **Isaiah 55:11**: "So shall my word be that goeth forth out of my mouth: it shall not return unto me void, but it shall accomplish that which I please, and it shall prosper in the thing whereto I sent it."

• **Isaiah 53:5**: "But he was wounded for our transgressions, he was bruised for our iniquities: the chastisement of our peace was upon him; and with his stripes we are healed."

• **2 Timothy 1:7**: "For God hath not given us the spirit of fear; but of power, and of love, and of a sound mind."

• **Ephesians 6:12**: "For we wrestle not against flesh and blood, but against principalities, against powers, against the rulers of the darkness of this world, against spiritual wickedness in high places."

• **Psalm 139:14**: "I will praise thee; for I am fearfully and wonderfully made: marvellous are thy works; and that my soul knoweth right well."

• **Philippians 4:4–8**: "Rejoice in the Lord alway: and again I say, Rejoice."

• **Isaiah 61:3**: "To appoint unto them that mourn in Zion, to give unto them beauty for ashes, the oil of joy for mourning, the garment of praise for the spirit of heaviness."

• **Psalm 42:5**: "Why art thou cast down, O my soul? and why art thou disquieted in me? hope thou in God: for I shall yet praise him for the help of his countenance."

Godly School Administrator & Staff

Society has **truly changed** over the last decade.

In times past, there was an **expectation** that those **responsible for our children** and overseeing our school system were of the **highest caliber—**

They upheld:

• **Good morals**

• **Strong leadership qualities**

We **felt safe** entrusting our children **to their care.**

Today, from the:

• **Principal**

• **Teacher**

• **Custodian**

• **Security personnel**

We **no longer know what to expect.**

Society has **shifted,** and an educator may come in one day **dressed as a man** and the next day **as a woman.**

Our children are now being taught about **"fluidity"**—it's **okay to be a boy today and a girl the next day.**

This behavior is not only **encouraged** but also **reinforced.**

To **stand firm** in the belief that **"I am created in the image of God; male and female, He created them"**—can now cause you to be viewed as **"the strange one."**

***

SPEAK THE ANSWER, NOT THE PROBLEM.

THE ANSWER IS THE WORD OF GOD

God, you are your Word.

Heavenly Father, we stand in agreement and speak over the lives of **every school administrator and staff member** involved in the lives of our children.

God, thank you for **Godly administrators, teachers, staff, cooks, security officers, janitors,** and all staff members who come in contact with our children.

• They **receive your wisdom.**

• Their **understanding comes from you.**

• They **acknowledge you** in all their ways.

• They **desire to hear you** and impart that knowledge to their students.

Thank you for staff who are **intercessors**—who, upon arrival to the school, **do a prayer walk** around the:

• **School grounds**

• **Classrooms**

• **Hallways**

• Who **plead the blood of Jesus** over the school.

• Who **call on angelic hosts** to be present.

• Who are **observant in the Holy Spirit** and can **block the plans of the enemy.**

• Who **discern when the enemy plans to release chaos** and **cancel those plans.**

• **You give them insight, foresight, and hindsight** as they deal with our children.

• You **reveal to them** the needs of our children and **how to reach them**

where they are.

• They are **perceptive and in tune** with the needs of the children.

You give them:

• **The right words**

• **The right approach**

• **The wisdom to reach the unreachable**

• **The ability to teach the unteachable**

• **The power to effect change** in the lives of those they serve.

They can **perceive, in the spirit realm,** which children are experiencing **chaotic lifestyles** and know **how to pray for change** in their lives.

Thank you for **strengthening the staff** and giving them **courage** to move forward.

The blood of Jesus covers them and keeps them **safe from harm.**

Bless them as they come and go throughout the school year.

Bless their families and finances.

Despite obstacles, bless them to remain **strong in their faith.**

May they **find ways** to show that **faith daily**—even as they **navigate legal challenges** surrounding their ability to **share your love** with students.

***

Scriptures for Meditation

• **1 John 1:1**: "That which was from the beginning, which we have heard, which we have seen with our eyes, which we have looked upon, and our hands have handled, of the Word of life."

• **Matthew 18:19–20**: "Again I say unto you, That if two of you shall agree on earth as touching any thing that they shall ask, it shall be done for them of my Father which is in heaven."

• **Proverbs 22:6**: "Train up a child in the way he should go: and when he is old, he will not depart from it."

• **Genesis 1:27**: "So God created man in his own image, in the image of God created he him; male and female created he them."

• **Psalm 32:8**: "I will instruct thee and teach thee in the way which thou shalt go: I will guide thee with mine eye."

• **Luke 12:11**: "And when they bring you unto the synagogues, and unto magistrates, and powers, take ye no thought how or what thing ye shall answer, or what ye shall say."

Elected Officials

SPEAK THE ANSWER, NOT THE PROBLEM.

Heavenly Father, we come in **obedience to your Word** and your **divine plan.**

You have **mandated us to pray** for those in authority:

> **1 Timothy 2:1–2**: *"I urge, then, first of all, that petitions, prayers, intercession, and thanksgiving be made for all people—for kings and all those in authority, that we may live peaceful and quiet lives in all godliness and holiness."*

We pray that our leaders will:

• **Know you, obey your statutes, and live godly lives.**

• **Do what is right** in your sight.

• **Fear and obey you** rather than man.

• **Uphold truth and justice.**

• Be **humble, courageous, kind, and compassionate.**

• **Seek your face** for wisdom in governing the people.

• Be **surrounded by wise counselors.**

• **Establish strong military rule** to protect your people and our nations.

• Let them be **unashamed** to declare their **love for you and for their country.**

• Let them **seek peace** on our behalf so that we may live **quiet and peaceful lives.**

***

Scriptures for Meditation

• **John 1:1**: "In the beginning was the Word, and the Word was with God, and the Word was God."

• **1 Timothy 2:1–2**: "I urge, then, first of all, that petitions, prayers, intercession, and thanksgiving be made for all people—for kings and all those in authority, that we may live peaceful and quiet lives in all godliness and holiness."

• **Proverbs 9:10**: "The fear of the Lord is the beginning of wisdom: and the knowledge of the holy is understanding."

• **Proverbs 3:5–7**: "Trust in the Lord with all thine heart; and lean not unto thine own understanding. In all thy ways acknowledge him, and he shall direct thy paths. Be not wise in thine own eyes: fear the Lord, and depart from evil."

• **1 Kings 15:11**: "And Asa did that which was right in the eyes of the Lord, as did David his father."

• **1 Kings 15:5**: "Because David did that which was right in the eyes of the Lord, and turned not aside from any thing that he commanded him all the days of his life, save only in the matter of Uriah the Hittite."

• **1 Kings 22:43**: "And he walked in all the ways of Asa his father; he turned not aside from it, doing that which was right in the eyes of the Lord."

Real Estate

Let me share a **quick testimony** with you.

My husband **passed away,** and I continued living in the home we had shared for **one year.**

One day, a situation occurred, and as I was talking to God about it, I **heard Him say clearly,**

"Move."

That was not the answer I had even **thought of** because I had been in the process of **remodeling our home** for a year prior to my husband's death.

I said to God,

"Move? But Lord, I don't get to enjoy all—"

And immediately, I had a **flashback** to **Lot's wife,** who was told **not to look back** as they were fleeing the city.

But she **disobeyed** and **lost her life.**

At that moment, I **immediately said,**

"Yes, Lord."

That was on **April 10, 2022.**

On that very day, I made calls to **banks and loan agents.**

I needed **two loans—One to refinance the home I was in and another to make a purchase**

I was told by both the **bank and the loan agent** that I **could not do both loans at the same time.**

They said,

"You need to do one at a time."

When God gives you an instruction,

No matter how **unlikely or strange** it may seem—**Just obey.**

I **obtained two loans,** located my **new home,** and signed the paperwork to move into my new home on **June 10, 2022.**

Exactly two months to the day that God instructed me to move.

The agent and everyone connected to the process were **amazed.**

***

SPEAK THE ANSWER, NOT THE PROBLEM.

God, you are the answer.

Heavenly Father, thank you for instructing me to **acknowledge you in everything I do.**

You give me **direct answers and instructions.**

I know your voice and will not second-guess your instructions.

You direct my path and guide me into the right decisions.

You know the right agent and the right location.

You give me the desires of my heart.

You have **made good plans** for me, and I **agree with your plans.**

I thank you that my property is exactly what someone is looking for.

It is in **pristine condition,** in the **right location,** and **priced fairly.**

I thank you that I am led to the **right property—**

It is in **pristine condition.**

It is in the **right location.**

It is **priced fairly.**

I **bless your holy name** and give you **glory** for your **faithfulness** and **goodness** to me.

I walk in **perfect alignment** with your Word.

***

Scriptures for Meditation

• **1 Samuel 15:22**: "And Samuel said, Hath the Lord as great delight in burnt offerings and sacrifices, as in obeying the voice of the Lord? Behold, to obey is better than sacrifice, and to hearken than the fat of rams."

• **Jeremiah 33:3**: "Call unto me, and I will answer thee, and show thee great and mighty things, which thou knowest not."

• **Proverbs 3:5–6**: "Trust in the Lord with all thine heart; and lean not unto thine own understanding. In all thy ways acknowledge him, and he shall direct thy paths."

• **John 10:28–30**: "And I give unto them eternal life; and they shall never perish, neither shall any man pluck them out of my hand."

• **Psalm 37:4–5**: "Delight thyself also in the Lord: and he shall give thee the desires of thine heart. Commit thy way unto the Lord; trust also in him; and he shall bring it to pass."

• **Jeremiah 29:11**: "For I know the thoughts that I think toward you, saith the Lord, thoughts of peace, and not of evil, to give you an expected end."

• **Lamentations 3:22–23**: "It is of the Lord's mercies that we are not consumed, because his compassions fail not. They are new every morning: great is thy faithfulness."

FINANCIAL

SPEAK THE ANSWER, NOT THE PROBLEM.

God, you are your Word.

Heavenly Father, I decree and declare that **it is my time to be blessed** according to your Word.

It is your will that I prosper and be in **good health,** even as my soul prospers.

I ask you for **wisdom to gain wealth** and for **understanding on how to multiply** all that you give to me.

Thank you for **enlightening my mind** with methods and techniques that bring **great wealth** to me.

Wealth and riches belong in my house.

I am a magnet for wealth, and it attaches itself to me.

I am a cheerful giver, and what I give **returns to me one hundredfold.**

I owe no man anything but to love them, as you have instructed me to do.

The more I bless others, the more I am blessed.

I am blessed going out and coming in.

Those who bless me are, in return, blessed.

Everything I touch prospers.

The windows of heaven are open to me.

Goodness and mercy are my friends and follow me closely.

I do not love money, but I acknowledge that **money answers every need** in my life.

Father, I thank you for revealing the **deep places of wealth** and placing that wealth in my hands.

Father, I thank you that the **wealth of the wicked** is being **turned over to me now.**

***

Scriptures for Meditation

• **John 1:1**: "In the beginning was the Word, and the Word was with God, and the Word was God."

• **Job 22:28–29**: "Thou shalt also decree a thing, and it shall be established unto thee: and the light shall shine upon thy ways."

• **Deuteronomy 28:6**: "Blessed shalt thou be when thou comest in, and blessed shalt thou be when thou goest out."

• **3 John 1:2–8**: "Beloved, I wish above all things that thou mayest prosper and be in health, even as thy soul prospereth."

• **Luke 6:38**: "Give, and it shall be given unto you; good measure, pressed down, and shaken together, and running over, shall men give into your bosom."

• **Genesis 12:3**: "And I will bless them that bless thee, and curse him that curseth thee: and in thee shall all families of the earth be blessed."

• **Romans 13:8**: "Owe no man anything, but to love one another: for he that loveth another hath fulfilled the law."

• **Psalm 112:3**: "Wealth and riches shall be in his house: and his righteousness endureth for ever."

• **Isaiah 43:3**: "For I am the Lord thy God, the Holy One of Israel, thy Saviour: I gave Egypt for thy ransom, Ethiopia and Seba for thee."

• **Proverbs 3:9–10**: "Honour the Lord with thy substance, and with the firstfruits of all thine increase: so shall thy barns be filled with plenty, and thy presses shall burst out with new wine."

LEGAL

SPEAK THE ANSWER, NOT THE PROBLEM.

God, you are your Word.

Heavenly Father, thank you for **wisdom** in knowing:

- **What to do**

- **When to do it**

- **How to address** the legal issue facing me

You are **fighting for me,** and I will **stand still** as you:

- **Identify and destroy** the enemy

- **Bring my case before you,** the righteous Judge

- **Judge between me and my enemy**

I thank you for uncovering the **hidden evidence** that will **vindicate me.**

You will overturn and overturn and give it to **whom it belongs.**

I decree and declare:

- **Everything that belongs to me** shall come quickly to me.

• **Everything stolen, misplaced, or hidden** from me will be **restored seven times.**

• **Everything that has been delayed** is being **released now in the name of**

Jesus.

• **Everything the enemy did to try to shake my faith** will surely **backfire.**

• **The favor of God** is flowing **so heavily upon me** that my **enemy will become afraid of me.**

For this cause,

• **I bow down before you.**

• **I lift up my hands and my voice.**

• **I give you mighty praise!**

***

Scriptures for Meditation

• **John 1:1**: "In the beginning was the Word, and the Word was with God, and the Word was God."

• **James 1:5**: "If any of you lack wisdom, let him ask of God, that giveth to all men liberally, and upbraideth not; and it shall be given him."

• **Exodus 14:14**: "The Lord shall fight for you, and ye shall hold your peace."

• **Psalm 7:11–12**: "God judgeth the righteous, and God is angry with the wicked every day."

• **2 Timothy 4:8**: "Henceforth there is laid up for me a crown of righteousness, which the Lord, the righteous judge, shall give me at that day: and not to me only, but unto all them also that love his appearing."

• **Ezekiel 21:27**: "I will overturn, overturn, overturn, it: and it shall be no more, until he come whose right it is; and I will give it him."

TRUST GOD
SCRIPTURES

Psalm 56:3–4 (Amplified Bible): *"When I am afraid, I will put my trust and faith in You. In God, whose word I praise; in God I have put my trust; I shall not fear. What can mere man do to me?"*

The Bible says that **God cannot lie.** He always keeps His promises, loves you, and has **good in store for you.** Trusting in Him means **believing what He says:**

• **About Himself**

• **About the world**

• **About you**

All that He says is true.

• **"Cast all your anxiety on Him because He cares for you."** *(1 Peter 5:7, NIV)*

• "You keep track of all my sorrows. You have collected all my tears in your bottle. You have recorded each one in Your book." *(Psalm 56:8, NLT)*

• "Rejoice always, pray continually, give thanks in all circumstances; for this is God's will for you in Christ Jesus." *(1 Thessalonians 5:16–18, NIV)*

• "Trust in the Lord with all your heart and lean not on your own understanding." *(Proverbs 3:5, NIV)*

• "And surely I am with you always, to the very end of the age." *(Matthew 28:20b, NIV)*

• "And my God will meet all your needs according to the riches of His glory in Christ Jesus." *(Philippians 4:19, NIV)*

• **Philippians 1:6 (KJV):** *"Being confident of this very thing, that he which hath begun a good work in you will perform it until the day of Jesus Christ."*

• **Philippians 1:6 (The Message Bible):** *"There has never been the slightest doubt in my mind that the God who started this great work in you would keep at it and bring it to a flourishing finish on the very day Christ Jesus appears."*

• **Psalm 34:1-22 (KJV):** *"I will bless the Lord at all times: his praise shall continually be in my mouth. My soul shall make her boast in the Lord: the* *humble shall hear thereof, and be glad. O magnify the Lord with me, and let us exalt his name together. I sought the Lord, and he heard me, and delivered me from all my fears. They looked unto him, and were lightened: and their faces were not ashamed. This poor man cried, and the Lord heard him, and saved him out of all his troubles. The angel of the Lord encampeth round about them that fear him, and delivereth them. O taste and see that the Lord is good: blessed is the man that trusteth in him. O fear the Lord, ye his saints: for there is no want to them that fear him. The young lions do lack, and suffer hunger: but they that seek the Lord shall not want any good thing. Come, ye children, hearken unto me: I will teach you the fear of the Lord. What man is he that desireth life, and loveth many days, that he may see good? Keep thy tongue from evil, and thy lips from speaking guile. Depart from evil, and do good; seek peace, and pursue it. The eyes of the Lord are upon the righteous, and his ears are open unto their cry. The face of the Lord is against them that do evil, to cut off the remembrance of them from the earth. The righteous cry, and the Lord heareth, and delivereth them out of all their troubles. The Lord is nigh unto them that are of a broken heart; and saveth such as be of a contrite spirit. Many are the afflictions of the righteous: but the Lord delivereth him out of them all. He keepeth all his bones: not one of them is broken. Evil shall slay the wicked: and they that hate the righteous shall be desolate. The Lord redeemeth the soul of his servants: and none of them that trust in him shall be desolate."*

Bind Up Ruling Spirits

SPEAK THE ANSWER, NOT THE PROBLEM.

THE ANSWER IS THE WORD OF GOD

Heavenly Father, we come **boldly to the throne of grace,** applying the **Blood of Jesus** over the enemy of **murder, violence, and death.**

Let God arise, and let His enemies be scattered today.

We render Satan helpless and powerless before the **Blood of Jesus.**

We bind up his powers, principalities, demonic spirits, and all **related spirits** in the name of **Jesus Christ.**

We call upon the warring angels to assist us and **break the power of darkness, death, and destruction—**

By the **power of Your shed blood**

By the **authority of Your Word**

We **cover and protect:**

• **Every home, block, neighborhood, city, state, country, and nation today.**

• **Every family member, church, and ministry.**

• **Our youth—may they walk in righteousness and safety.**

We **bind up domestic violence**—including in the pulpit and church.

We **bind up child abuse** and claim Your **promises of protection** in:

• **Psalm 91**

• **Isaiah 54:17**

• **Exodus 12:13**

We **loose the spirit of:**

• **Love**

• **Peace**

• **Compassion**

• **Hope**

• **Abundant life**

For **ourselves, everyone connected to us, and all who are connected to them.**

We lift up:

• **Every gang leader, gang member, drug dealer, murderer, rapist,** thief, and liar before You today.

• Let the spirit of repentance and conviction rain down upon them.

Reveal their hiding places and their plots.

Confuse their tongues and send disarray into their camp.

Let every evil plan backfire.

If they refuse to repent and turn away, let the angels of the Lord chase them down a dark, slippery path, fill them with delusions, and give them no rest or peace.

God, transform the hearts and minds of those bound by the enemy.

We pull down strongholds today and decree righteousness in the earthly realm.

Cover every police officer and law enforcement person with the Blood of Jesus.

Give them clarity, wisdom, and direction in their duties.

Keep them safe, and prevent errors in judgment.

We bind up police brutality and declare that every act of unrighteousness will be exposed.

We pray for **leaders**—

Grant them insight, foresight, wisdom, and understanding to combat crime.

We call upon the **ministering angels** to:

• **Minister to all affected by violence.**

• **Cover them with Your love.**

• **Be their strength and help today.**

• **Bring them comfort in Jesus' name.**

We **commit these things into Your hands.**

We bow down and worship You for Your mighty and marvelous works.

It takes faith to believe, and we decree and declare that we believe.

We are safe and confident in You, knowing that ALL POWER BELONGS TO YOU.

***

Scriptures for Meditation

• **John 1:1**: *"In the beginning was the Word, and the Word was with God, and the Word was God."*

- **Exodus 12:13**: *"And the blood shall be to you for a token upon the houses where ye are: and when I see the blood, I will pass over you, and the plague shall not be upon you to destroy you, when I smite the land of Egypt."*

- **Matthew 18:18**: *"Verily I say unto you, Whatsoever ye shall bind on earth shall be bound in heaven: and whatsoever ye shall loose on earth shall be loosed in heaven."*

- **Luke 10:19**: *"Behold, I give unto you power to tread on serpents and scorpions, and over all the power of the enemy: and nothing shall by any means hurt you."*

- **Hebrews 1:14**: *"Are they not all ministering spirits, sent forth to minister for them who shall be heirs of salvation?"*

- **Revelation 12:11**: *"And they overcame him by the blood of the Lamb, and by the word of their testimony; and they loved not their lives unto the death."*

- **Psalm 95:1–6**: *"O come, let us sing unto the Lord: let us make a joyful noise to the rock of our salvation. Let us come before his presence with thanksgiving, and make a joyful noise unto him with psalms."*

- **Psalm 62:10**: *"Trust not in oppression, and become not vain in robbery: if riches increase, set not your heart upon them."*

MISSING PERSON

Almost every day there is news of someone disappearing, being kidnapped or even perhaps runaways. This prayer is for those who are missing.

***

SPEAK THE ANSWER, NOT THE PROBLEM.

Your Word is the answer, and You are Your Word.

Heavenly Father,

We come to Your throne on behalf of every person who is missing. In accordance with Your Word, we pray for our families, sons, daughters, and all those whose whereabouts are unknown. **Your eyes see everything.** Nothing is hidden from You.

If they are being held captive, we stand on Your promise:

"Shall the prey be taken from the mighty, or the lawful captive delivered? But thus saith the Lord: Even the captives of the mighty shall be taken away, and the prey of the terrible shall be delivered: for I will contend with him that contendeth with thee, and I will save thy children." (Isaiah 49:24–25)

We decree and declare that You are sending in the **SWAT team of warring angels** to go in, **rescue them,** and snatch them from the hands of the enemy.

Give them supernatural strength and courage to call upon Your name.

Send ministering angels to comfort and sustain them in these difficult days.

For those who have **run away** and are now trapped in dangerous situations:

• **Make a way of escape.**

• **Blind the eyes of their captors.**

• **Cause them to forget to lock doors, follow routines, or secure restraints.**

• **Give the captives divine wisdom** to recognize the right moment to flee.

We pray that:

• **Neighbors and witnesses** will become suspicious and have the courage to report their concerns.

• **The one holding them captive** will become careless, boastful, and reckless—causing their own exposure.

• **Vital information** will reach the right ears in law enforcement—the **FBI, DEA, Secret Service, and local authorities.**

We cry out against the **dark networks of human trafficking, sex trafficking, kidnapping, and body snatching.**

Expose those in high places who take part in these wicked acts.

Bring every hidden thing into the light.

Tear down the strongholds of oppression, and **let the captives be set free.**

Father, we will cry out to You on their behalf until You bring them home safely.

***

Scriptures for Declaration

• **John 1:1** – *"In the beginning was the Word, and the Word was with God, and the Word was God."*

• **Hebrews 4:16** – *"Let us therefore come boldly unto the throne of grace, that we may obtain mercy, and find grace to help in time of need."*

• **Nehemiah 4:14** – *"Be not afraid of them: remember the Lord, which is great and terrible, and fight for your brethren, your sons, and your daughters, your wives, and your houses."*

• **Proverbs 15:3** – *"The eyes of the Lord are in every place, beholding the evil and the good."*

• **Job 22:28–29** – *"Thou shalt also decree a thing, and it shall be established unto thee: and the light shall shine upon thy ways."*

• **Psalm 91:11–12** – *"For he shall give his angels charge over thee, to keep thee in all thy ways. They shall bear thee up in their hands, lest thou dash thy foot against a stone."*

• **Hebrews 1:14** – *"Are they not all ministering spirits, sent forth to minister for them who shall be heirs of salvation?"*

• **John 12:40** – *"He hath blinded their eyes, and hardened their heart; that they should not see with their eyes, nor understand with their heart, and be converted, and I should heal them."*

• **Jeremiah 31:15** – *"Thus saith the Lord; A voice was heard in Ramah, lamentation, and bitter weeping; Rachel weeping for her children refused to be comforted for her children, because they were not."*

• **Isaiah 43:6** – *"I will say to the north, Give up; and to the south, Keep not back: bring my sons from far, and my daughters from the ends of the earth."*

Pray For Those Behind Prison Doors

SPEAK THE ANSWER, NOT THE PROBLEM.

The answer is Your Word. God, You are Your Word.

Heavenly Father,

We **stand in the gap** for those behind prison bars. We may not understand **why they are there,** but You **know all things** and have a **purpose for allowing it to be so.**

We believe Your Word and speak into their lives—

There is no place too far, too hidden, or too dark for Your Spirit to reach them. *(Psalm 139:8)*

Though they are behind locked doors, their spirits are not bound.

We **plead the Blood of Jesus** over their:

• **Lives**

• **Minds**

• **Bodies**

• **Souls**

• **Spirits**

Thank You, God, for **disrupting the enemy's plans** for their demise.

Thank You for **bringing them to a place of humility** where they will **come to themselves** and realize there is **no help outside of You.** *(Luke 15:17)*

Thank You, God, for drawing them to You.

Now they will call on Your Name, and You will hear them. *(Romans 10:13)*

Now they will stop and reflect on their mistakes.

Now You will create in them a clean heart and renew their mind. *(Psalm 51:10)*

Now the weight of their sin will awaken them to the need for change.

Now they will seek Your face with sincerity and hunger for righteousness.

We decree and declare:

• Every **prayer they have heard** will rise in their spirit.

• Every **sermon spoken over them** will come alive in their hearts.

• Every **prophetic word spoken over their lives** will take root.

• The **fragrance of prayer** will fill their environment and surround them with hope.

Father, we pray for those **who are innocent:**

• **Bring forth the evidence** that will prove their innocence and set them free.

• **Let justice prevail** over injustice.

• **Expose all corruption, misconduct, and false accusations.**

• **Call forth all DNA evidence and hidden proof.**

• **Destroy every false testimony and crumbling foundation of injustice.**

We decree and declare this is a season where **many innocent prisoners shall be set free.**

Father, we pray for those **who are guilty as charged:**

• **Let them come to a place of true repentance.**

• **Let godly sorrow overwhelm them** and cause them to turn from sin. *(2 Corinthians 7:10)*

• **Give them a spiritual heart transplant.** *(Ezekiel 36:26)*

• **Give them a renewed mind that seeks salvation.** *(Romans 12:2)*

***

Scriptures for Declaration

• **John 1:1** – *"In the beginning was the Word, and the Word was with God, and the Word was God."*

• **Matthew 25:31–46** – *"I was in prison, and you came to visit me."*

• **Psalm 139:8** – *"If I ascend up into heaven, thou art there: if I make my bed in hell, behold, thou art there."*

• **Genesis 16:13** – *"Thou God seest me."*

• **Romans 10:13** – *"For whosoever shall call upon the name of the Lord shall be saved."*

• **Psalm 51:10** – *"Create in me a clean heart, O God; and renew a right spirit within me."*

• **Hebrews 13:1–3** – *"Remember those in prison as if you were bound with them."*

• **Matthew 25:34–40** – *"Whatever you did for the least of these, you did for Me."*

• **Genesis 41:14–16** – *Joseph was taken from prison and placed before the king.*

• **Psalm 105:19–21** – *"The word of the Lord tried him, until the appointed time of his release."*

• **Psalm 69:33** – *"For the Lord heareth the poor, and despiseth not his prisoners."*

• **Isaiah 61:1–3** – *"To proclaim liberty to the captives, and the opening of the prison to them that are bound."*

Prayers Against Violence

SPEAK THE ANSWER, NOT THE PROBLEM.

THE ANSWER IS THE WORD OF GOD.

Heavenly Father,

We come into **agreement with intercessors across the land,** binding up the **spirit of murder, suicide, and violence.**

We plead the Blood of Jesus over:

• Every **home, block, neighborhood, and city.**

• Every **family, individual, and community in need of protection.**

Your Word declares, "Thou shalt not kill" *(Exodus 20:13)*—so we stand on this truth and **rebuke the forces of darkness.**

We loose Your love, caring, compassion, safety, and peace.

Your Word says You have ordained peace for Your people. *(Isaiah 26:12)*

You came that **we may have abundant life** *(John 10:10)*, and so:

• **We declare abundant life over our families and communities.**

• **No weapon formed against us will prosper.** *(Isaiah 54:17)*

• **You save us from the violent man.** *(Psalm 18:48)*

• **You hide us under the shadow of Your wings.** *(Psalm 91:4)*

• **Your name is a strong tower; we run to You and are safe.** *(Proverbs 18:10)*

We bind the strongman of violence and render him **helpless before the Blood of Jesus.**

We ask for a divine restraining order against the **spirit of murder, violence, and rape.**

We send confusion to the enemy's camp.

We cancel every attack, scheme, plot, and plan of the enemy.

We pray that:

• **Those who set out to rob, beat, and harm others** will **fall into their own traps.** *(Psalm 35:8)*

• **Those who have hidden criminals in the past** will **no longer do so.**

• **By their own words, they will be exposed and condemned.** *(Matthew 12:37)*

Father, **You see their gathering places** where they meet to plot evil.

Let their plans be revealed to authorities before they can act.

Let their words reach the ears of the police, FBI, DEA, and law enforcement.

Let their weapons malfunction, their stolen cars break down, and their timing be confused.

We superimpose Your will and Your purpose over the plans of the enemy **in Jesus' name.**

Give us discernment to sense when things are wrong.

Reveal every hidden thing so that we, the intercessors, will know how to pray.

We disrupt the plans of the enemy before harm can be done.

Your eyes see everything—nothing is hidden from You. *(Proverbs 15:3)*

We declare that all power belongs to You. *(Revelation 19:1)*

• **You are able to keep us safe from those plotting against us.** *(Psalm 121:7)*

***

Scriptures for Declaration

• **Matthew 18:18–19** – *"Verily I say unto you, Whatsoever ye shall bind on earth shall be bound in heaven: and whatsoever ye shall loose on earth shall be loosed in heaven."*

• **Exodus 12:13** – *"And when I see the blood, I will pass over you, and the plague shall not be upon you to destroy you."*

• **Exodus 20:13** – *"Thou shalt not kill."*

• **John 13:34–35** – *"A new commandment I give unto you, That ye love one another; as I have loved you, that ye also love one another."*

• **Matthew 19:19** – *"Honor thy father and thy mother: and, Thou shalt love thy neighbor as thyself."*

• **Psalm 4:8** – *"I will both lay me down in peace, and sleep: for thou, Lord, only makest me dwell in safety."*

• **Proverbs 16:7** – *"When a man's ways please the Lord, he maketh even his enemies to be at peace with him."*

- **Psalm 18:48** – *"He delivereth me from mine enemies: yea, thou liftest me up above those that rise up against me: thou hast delivered me from the violent man."*

- **Matthew 12:29** – *"Or else how can one enter into a strong man's house, and spoil his goods, except he first bind the strong man? And then he will spoil his house."*

- **John 10:10** – *"The thief cometh not, but for to steal, and to kill, and to destroy: I am come that they might have life, and that they might have it more abundantly."*

- **Revelation 19:1** – *"Alleluia; Salvation, and glory, and honour, and power, unto the Lord our God."*

- **2 Chronicles 20:12** – *"O our God, wilt thou not judge them? for we have no might against this great company that cometh against us; neither know we what to do: but our eyes are upon thee."*

Prayer of Deliverance

Do you know anyone who suffers from **delusions, paranoia, anxiety, major depression, oppression, paralyzing fear, abandonment,** and a **state of continued frustration**? Do you know someone who is **so overwhelmed with fear** that they refuse to leave their home? It can be **heartbreaking** to watch someone struggling with these issues.

What do you do? What can you do? Do you feel **your hands are tied** and there is nothing you can do? What if that person **does not recognize**—and, in most cases, they will not—that they need deliverance?

Take time to read these **accounts of deliverance** from **demonic possession**:

• **Matthew 17:14–21** and **Mark 9:14–29** (The father bringing his child to be delivered).

• **Matthew 8:28–34** and **Mark 5:1–20** (The healing of two demon-possessed men).

• **Matthew 15:21–28** and **Mark 7:24–30** (The healing of the Canaanite woman's daughter).

I am not saying that all of the above-mentioned conditions are the result of **demonic possession.** However, they are **not of God** and are the **result of Satan's influence and interference.**

The purpose of these chapters is to **build your faith** in knowing that **no matter the circumstances,** *nothing is impossible for God*—not even when the person does **not recognize their need for deliverance.**

Your hands **are not tied.**

It is **not a hopeless situation.**

There is deliverance.

"This kind goes out by fasting and prayer." (Matthew 17:21)

This kind requires a **two-punch combination.** There is a saying: *You must want help in order to be helped.* This is generally true, but there is always **an exception to the rule.** In this case, the exception is **intercession.**

I encourage you to:

• **Apply the Blood of Jesus.**
• **Apply the Word.**

• **Stand on it.**

• **Fast and pray.**

Do not be deceived by **what you see, hear, or feel.**

The Word of God works.

The Blood of Jesus works.

So **activate your faith** and **dare to intercede.**

Release this **prayer of deliverance again, and again, and again** until **God's truth manifests** in the life of the person you are interceding for

***

SPEAK THE ANSWER, NOT THE PROBLEM.

GOD'S WORD IS THE ANSWER

In the name of Jesus, I declare that **whom the Son sets free is free indeed.** I decree and declare **liberty** from **delusional spirits, paranoia, anxiety, depression, oppression, fear, abandonment, and frustration.**

I bind up **nervous breakdown** and **mental breaks from reality.** I come against **confusion in the mind.**

I break the lingering effects of **drugs, alcoholism, and addiction.** The **attack of the enemy against your mind is canceled.**

I speak **power, love, and a sound mind.** Let **the mind of Christ be in you.** Be **transformed by the renewing of your mind.**

Perfect love casts out fear. Let the **perfect love of Jesus saturate your mind.** You will **come into agreement with the Word of God.**

I decree and declare that **the Word of God will be manifested in your life.**

The **anointing of God** not only **breaks but destroys every yoke.**

I speak that **the snare is broken, and you make your way of escape.**

The **walls of defeat** fall down, and you step over into your **freedom.**

I say to the enemy:

You will not destroy my child, my grandchild, or anyone connected to me.

You will not destroy their destiny.

In the **name of Jesus,** I decree and declare **freedom from the hand of the enemy.**

Let the **mind be regulated.**

Let them become **rooted and established** in Your **Word.**

Let their **thinking come into alignment** with Your Word—those things that are:

• **True**

• **Honest**

• **Just**

• **Pure**

• **Lovely**

• **Of good report** *(Philippians 4:8)*

I speak **overcoming power** and **victorious living** into their lives.

I declare that **your pain and shame shall become your platform to bring others to deliverance.**

The **Blood of Jesus** and the **Word of God** operate in the mind and **bring deliverance now.**

The **peace of God** rests, rules, and abides **in the name of Jesus.**

I **declare and decree: It is so!**

It **shall manifest**, and we **give glory to God**, Almighty God, **strong deliverer**, the One who has **all power** in His **hand and in His name.**

Thanks be to **our God**, who is **bigger than anything we face** and has the power to speak **deliverance and victory** into any situation.

For this cause, we **bow our knees to You,**

humble ourselves before You,

lift up our voices in praise,

and **worship You, our Lord, our God, our Savior.**

> **Isaiah 26:3**: *"Thou wilt keep him in perfect peace, whose mind is stayed on thee: because he trusteth in thee."*

***

Other Scriptures for Meditation:

• **2 Timothy 1:7**: "For God hath not given us the spirit of fear; but of power, and of love, and of a sound mind."

• **Philippians 2:5**: "Let this mind be in you, which was also in Christ Jesus."

• **Romans 12:2**: "And be not conformed to this world: but be ye transformed by the renewing of your mind, that ye may prove what is that good, and acceptable, and perfect, will of God."

• **Philippians 4:7**: "And the peace of God, which passeth all understanding, shall keep your hearts and minds through Christ Jesus."

• **1 Peter 1:13**: "Wherefore gird up the loins of your mind, be sober, and hope to the end for the grace that is to be brought unto you at the revelation of Jesus Christ."

• **1 John 4:18**: "There is no fear in love; but perfect love casteth out fear: because fear hath torment. He that feareth is not made perfect in love."

• **1 Corinthians 2:16**: "For who hath known the mind of the Lord, that he may instruct him? But we have the mind of Christ."

• **Philippians 4:8**: "Finally, brethren, whatsoever things are true, whatsoever things are honest, whatsoever things are just, whatsoever things are pure, whatsoever things are lovely, whatsoever things are of good report; if there be any virtue, and if there be any praise, think on these things."

• **Hebrews 4:12**: "For the word of God is quick, and powerful, and sharper than any twoedged sword, piercing even to the dividing asunder of soul and spirit, and of the joints and marrow, and is a discerner of the thoughts and intents of the heart."

THE POWER OF DECREES

Who can make decrees?

A **decree** is an **official order issued by a legal authority.** To **declare** means to **make something known formally and officially.**

Speak the scriptures out loud. A decree is taking **God's words** and **speaking them out.** We have been given **authority from Jesus** to make these **decrees** into our realms of influence, and as we do so, we begin to **create the will of God in our lives** in the **spiritual realm.**

We become that **royal scepter of authority** in our **Father's hand,** as we **legislate the laws of our Kingdom,** enforcing them—

"on earth as it is in heaven."

We **rule in the midst of our enemies.**

Satan tempted Jesus **over and over.** Jesus **always responded** with:

"It is written..."

Then, He would **quote scripture.**

When we **return God's word to Him,** angels are **released** to carry out the **fulfillment of the scripture.**

"Praise the LORD, you angels of his, you powerful warriors who carry out his decrees and obey his orders!" *(Psalm 103:20, NET Bible)*

A **decree** carries the **weight of a court order.**

• The **decree starts** with a **statement of what will happen.**

• The **decree institutes** the **power, will, and purpose of God.**

• **Decrees** post a **judgment against the enemy.**

• **Decrees** give us **favor** against the enemy.

• The **enemy has no power** to **change our decree.**

Decrees bring us into alignment with God's words.

This is where you **use your faith** to bring forth **decrees** in your life.

Faith enables us to **see what is unseen** and cause it to **come forth.**

At the same time, it allows us to **see what is** and declare that it **will not be.**

We **use our mouth** to **speak things into our reality.**

We decree:

• **Our household is saved.**

• **Our marriages are strong.**

• **We have more than enough.**

"Thou shalt also decree a thing, and it shall be established unto thee: and the light shall shine upon thy ways." *(Job 22:28)*

What Is a Decree?

Webster defines **decree** as:

1. **An order usually having the force of law.**

2. **A religious ordinance enacted by a council or titular head.**

3. **A foreordaining will.**

In other words, a **decree** is an **official order issued by a legal authority.**

To **make a decree,** you must have the **legal authority** to do so.

We have been **given authority from Jesus** to make **decrees** with the **expectation** that they shall be **established in our lives.**

To **declare** means to **make something known formally and officially.**

What good would a **decree** be if it was **not made known** to others?

Do All Decrees Stand?

Can you **make any type of decree** you wish and **expect God to back you up?**

No. Your **decree** must **line up with the Word of God.**

A **decree** is taking **God's word** and **speaking it out loud.**

Issuing a decree is not based on **your words, thoughts, desires, or wishes.**

The **decree** must be based on the **foundational truth of God's word.**

That is why **He—God—will establish it.**

It is **His own words.**

When we **return God's word to Him,** angels are **released** to carry out the **fulfillment of the scripture.**

"Praise the LORD, you angels of his, you powerful warriors who carry out his decrees and obey his orders!" *(Psalm 103:20)*

DECREES OVER OUR CHILDREN

Children often have **word curses** spoken over their lives—words like:

"You are stupid."

"You are ugly."

"You will never be anything."

"You are just like your mother or father."

These words may be spoken **out of anger, frustration, bitterness, or hurt.**

The old saying, **"Sticks and stones may break my bones, but words will never hurt me,"** is **only partly true.**

Words can **break the heart.**

Words can **break the spirit.**

It is time to **break generational curses** and **release generational blessings** over our children.

I decree and declare that **our children are:**

• **Protected by the Blood of Jesus.**

• Angels surround them to keep them from harm and danger. *(Psalm 91, Psalm 34:7)*

• **Blessed with abundant life.** *(John 10:10)*

• **Lovers of the Lord with all their heart.** *(Matthew 22:37)*

• **Serving Him with all their might.** *(Matthew 22:37)*

• **Walking in obedience.** *(Luke 11:28)*

• **Hearing the voice of God.** *(1 Samuel 3:4)*

• **A blessing to others.** *(Psalm 127:3–5)*

• **Receiving wisdom.** *(Proverbs 19:23)*

• **Having a teachable spirit.** *(Proverbs 19:23)*

• **The head and not the tail.** *(Deuteronomy 28:13)*

• **Above and not beneath.** *(Deuteronomy 28:13)*

• **Blessed coming in and going out.** *(Deuteronomy 28:6)*

• **Not ensnared by the enemy.** *(Psalm 124:7–8)*

• **Free from alcohol and drugs.** *(Proverbs 20:1)*

• **Freed from generational curses of poverty, homelessness, and lawlessness.** *(Deuteronomy 28)*

- **Neither participants nor victims of violence.** *(Proverbs 1:15–19)*

- **Protected in what they see and hear.** *(Psalm 101:3)*

- **Surrounded by favor.** *(Psalm 5:12)*

- **Favored by everyone they come in contact with.** *(Psalm 147:11)*

- **Surrounded by Godly laborers and mentors.** *(Matthew 9:37–38)*

- **Loving to do what is right in the sight of God.** *(Psalm 119:9–11)*

- **Healthy and strong.** *(3 John 1:3)*

- **Compassionate and generous.** *(Luke 6:38)*

- **Used by God at a young age.** *(1 Samuel 3:4)*

- **Growing in their love for God and seeking to know Him.** *(1 Samuel 3:4)*

- **Blessed in every area of their lives.** *(Deuteronomy 28)*

- **A blessing to all around them.** *(Genesis 12:2)*

- **Overcomers of every scheme the enemy tries to bring against them.** *(John 14:4)*

- **Stable and secure in life.** *(Isaiah 33:6)*

We **reject** every **negative word** spoken over our children and **replace** it with the **Word of God.**

We **decree and declare** that they will **rise above** every obstacle, walk in **their divine purpose,** and **fulfill their God-ordained destiny.**

May their lives be **filled with God's favor, peace, and power.**

"Death and life are in the power of the tongue, and those who love it will eat its fruit." *(Proverbs 18:21)*

"These decrees were written on behalf of my grandson shortly after his birth. Take them, speak them, and rewrite them specifically for your loved ones."

- Intercessor Yvonne Perkins

MY PRAYER AND DECREES FOR GRANDCHILDREN

• _____ is blessed and highly favored by God. *(Ephesians 1:11, Psalm 84:4)*

• _____ loves God with all of her/his heart, mind, body, soul, and might. *(Matthew 22:37–40)*

• _____ hears the voice of God. *(John 10:27, 1 Samuel 3:7–10)*

• _____ acknowledges God in all ways. *(Proverbs 3:5–6)*

• _____ delights in the Lord. *(Psalm 37:4)*

• _____ lives a surrendered and yielded life. *(Romans 12:1)*

• _____ is mightily used by God. *(2 Timothy 2:21–26)*

• _____ is now and will continue to walk in the destiny that God has for him/her. *(Jeremiah 29:11)*

- _____ does not allow anyone or anything to interfere with his/her relationship with God.

- _____ forgives himself/herself easily for any mistakes or misjudgments made. *(1 John 1:9)*

- _____ holds no resentment, bitterness, or unforgiveness toward anyone. *(Ephesians 4:31–5:2)*

- _____ is courageous, bold, and determined to grow in the knowledge and work of God. *(Psalm 25:4)*

- _____ knows and is continually discovering his/her purpose in life.

- _____ walks in humility before a loving God. *(James 4:10)*

I speak the answer over _____'s life. I declare Your word, God, that the above decrees are true and established in _____'s life.

I decree that every self-defeating word and plan of the enemy is overthrown. _____'s heart is open before You as he/she allows You to examine him/her and take him/her to a place of honest self-examination.

You have called _____ to this place to be in Your presence and to hear directly from You. Speak, God, to _____'s heart.

Help _____ face everything in his/her life that he/she does not want to face—every hurt, pain, anger, sadness, and grief—and call it out by name. In doing so, You will set _____ free from the past and launch him/her into his/her future.

This life-changing experience will fast-forward _____ into the exact **Kairos time** he/she is meant to be in. *(Kairos describes the appointed time of the purpose of God.)*

DECREES FOR FAVOR

SPEAK THE ANSWER, NOT THE PROBLEM.

THE ANSWER IS THE WORD OF GOD.

Heavenly Father, I decree and declare favor over my life, my home, and all connections to me. I declare that I have the desires of my heart because I delight myself in the things of God.

Psalm 5:12: "For thou, LORD, wilt bless the righteous; with favour wilt thou compass him as with a shield."

Psalm 41:11: "By this I know that thou favourest me, because mine enemy doth not triumph over me."

Psalm 90:17: "Let the favor of the Lord our God be upon us, and establish the work of our hands upon us; yes, establish the work of our hands!"

Psalm 30:5: "For his anger lasts only a moment, but his favor lasts a lifetime; weeping may stay for the night, but rejoicing comes in the morning."

Psalm 84:11: "For the LORD God is a sun and shield; the LORD bestows favor and honor; no good thing does he withhold from those whose walk is blameless."

Psalm 106:4-5: "Remember me, LORD, when you show favor to your people, come to my aid when you save them, that I may enjoy the prosperity of your chosen ones, that I may share in the joy of your nation and join your inheritance in giving praise."

Esther 2:8-9: "She pleased him and won his favor. Immediately he provided her with her beauty treatments and special food. He assigned to her seven female attendants selected from the king's palace and moved her and her attendants into the best place in the harem."

DECREES FOR DEPRESSION

SPEAK THE ANSWER, NOT THE PROBLEM.

THE ANSWER IS THE WORD OF GOD

Heavenly Father, we come asking You to release the Blood of Jesus over every person dealing with depression. The **39 stripes** on Your body guarantee our healing—healing for the body, mind, will, spirit, and emotions.

We come against the power of darkness that brings pain, torment, sorrow, guilt, and shame. We receive the **abundant life** that You have ordained.

We **speak to the chemicals** in the brain that they become regulated and function as they should. We speak to **norepinephrine, serotonin, and dopamine**—we declare that these neurotransmitters function normally.

The Holy Spirit **changes our appetite** and teaches us how to eat nutritious meals and prepare our food properly.

We now **respond to and stand on Your Word**: **"Rejoice! Again, I say rejoice."**

God, give us **a mind to worship You**. As we spend time in worship, You will heal our mind, will, emotions, and spirit.

We **change our garments** and put on the **garment of praise**:

> ***Psalm 42:11:*** *"Why are you cast down, O my soul? And why are you disquieted within me? Hope in God: for I shall yet praise Him, who is the health of my countenance, and my God."*

I **decree and declare: I will not die but live and declare the works of God.**

I decree and declare that your soul shall no longer be in turmoil, for your hope is in God.

The 39 stripes on Jesus' back secured your physical, emotional, mental, and spiritual healing; therefore, be healed in the name of Jesus.

I decree and declare that the shed blood of Jesus will flow through your body and cause any chemical imbalance to come into alignment with the Word of God.

Your heart will be open to receive words of healing; your eyes of understanding will be open to see the brighter days ahead; your ears will be open to hear and comprehend the truth, and it shall set you free.

We bind up anything that stands in the way of walking out of the dark, hopeless hole of depression and into the marvelous light of God's Word.

I decree and declare that laughter will fill your world, and hope will abound as you take off the garment of pain, heaviness, and sorrow and put on the garment of praise and joy.

I decree and declare that the yoke-destroying anointing of God is even now destroying the work of the enemy. Let the soil of your heart be plowed, open, and ready to receive the seed of life.

I decree and declare it is so in the name of Jesus, and it shall not be any other way. Receive the abundant life of Jesus as He heals your emotions today.

DECREES FOR A JOB

Bishop H. W. Goldberry would make this declaration before preaching:

"The devil is a liar. I believe God. Jesus is here. I'm gonna have just what I want by the power, the authority, and the ability of the Almighty God, in the name of Jesus!"

***

SPEAK THE ANSWER, NOT THE PROBLEM.

THE ANSWER IS THE WORD OF GOD

God, You are Your Word.

Heavenly Father, we stand in agreement and make the following decrees for a job:

• **God is giving me the desires of my heart because I delight myself in Him.**

• I will have the job/career that I desire.

• Favor rests upon me, and even when I don't meet the qualifications for the job at the present time, I will still have that job.

• I will have the hours that I want.

• I will have the location that I want.

• I command my salary, and it is established.

• I have favor with the CEO, supervisors, and co-workers.

• Job positions are created just for me.

• I have witty ideas that cause me to get ahead on the job.

• I command the right salary.

• I will have every benefit, including sick days, vacation, and personal business days.

• I am the best of the best, and my abilities are recognized by those in authority.

• Doors and job opportunities are open for me.

• I am a light on my job, and the job environment is blessed because I am

there.

• It is as I decree it to be, and it shall not be any other way in the name of Jesus.

DECREES FOR HEALING

What Does the Word of God Say About Healing?

Isaiah 53:5: *"But He was wounded for our transgressions, He was bruised for our iniquities; The chastisement for our peace was upon Him, and by His stripes we are healed."*

1 Peter 2:24: *"He Himself bore our sins in His body on the tree, so that we may be delivered from sin and live in righteousness; by His stripes, you were healed."*

When you study the Word of God, you will notice that **the Word backs up the Word.** In the Old Testament, Isaiah looks into the future and declares, *"by the stripes of Jesus, we are healed."* In the New Testament, Peter confirms this truth, declaring, *"we were healed."*

By His Stripes

Whipping was a common form of punishment in biblical times. It was customary to administer **no more than 40 lashes**, depending on the crime committed.

> **Deuteronomy 25:3**: *"Forty stripes may be given him, but not more, lest, if one should go on to beat him with more stripes than these, your brother be degraded in your sight."*

Paul spoke of being whipped **39 times**:

> **2 Corinthians 11:23-25**: *"Are they servants of Christ? (I am talking like a madman.) I am a better one—with far greater labors, far more imprisonments, with countless beatings, and often near death. Five times I received at the hands of the Jews the forty lashes less one."*

The whip used was described as a **short whip** made of **three or more leather straps** connected to a handle. The leather straps were knotted with weights at the end and embedded with **metal, nails, and bone shards**—often using sharp fragments from the knucklebone of a sheep.

I encourage you to read these resources that provide medical insights into the crucifixion of Jesus Christ:

• **"The Science of the Crucifixion"** by Cahleen Shrier, Ph.D., Professor in the Department of Biology and Chemistry

• **"A Physician's View of the Crucifixion of Jesus Christ"** by Dr. C. Truman Davis

• **"The Anatomical & Physiological Details of Death by Crucifixion"** by Vince Miller

> **Isaiah 52:14**: *"As many were astonished at thee; his visage was so marred more than any man, and his form more than the sons of men.*

The **New Living Translation** describes Jesus' suffering as follows:

> *"But many were amazed when they saw him. His face was so disfigured he seemed hardly human, and from his appearance, one would scarcely know he was a man."*

The word **"marred"** means **disfigured**.

Why Is This Important?

I share this to **paint a picture** of what Jesus Christ endured on our behalf—to **fulfill the Word of God** and **provide healing** for those who trust in Him. The stripes on Jesus' body, the crown of thorns on His head, the nails in His hands and feet, and the piercing in His side represent the **entire body**.

There is no disease—known or unknown to man, created by nature or in a lab, physical or mental—that God cannot heal.

Examples of Healing in the Bible

The Bible contains **numerous** examples of healing. I encourage you to read these accounts to strengthen your faith:

Physical Healing (Leprosy, blindness, paralysis, and other infirmities)

• *Mark 1:40-42*

• *Matthew 8:14-15*

• *Matthew 9:2-7*

• *Matthew 9:20-22*

• *Luke 8:43-48*

Healing of the Mind and Spirit (Deliverance from oppression and demonic influences)

- *Matthew 15:21-28*

- *Matthew 17:14-18*

- *Luke 9:38-43*

- *Mark 8:22-26*

- *Mark 7:31-37*

- *John 4:46-54*

- *John 5:1-9*

- *Mark 1:23-26*

What Does It Take to Receive Your Healing?

Faith is key to receiving healing.

- **Mark 5:34**: *"Jesus said to her, 'Daughter, your faith has made you well; go in peace, and be healed of your disease.'"*

- **Matthew 9:22**: *"Jesus said to the woman with the issue of blood, 'Your faith has healed you.'"*

- **Luke 17:19**: *"Jesus said to the leper, 'Your faith has made you well.'"*

- **Luke 18:42**: *"Jesus said to a blind beggar, 'Your faith has made you well.'"*

***

SPEAK THE ANSWER, NOT THE PROBLEM.

THE ANSWER IS THE WORD OF GOD. GOD, YOU ARE YOUR WORD.

Heavenly Father, I decree and declare healing in the name of Your Son, Jesus.

You are Jehovah-Rapha. *(Exodus 15:26)*

"Heal me, O Lord, and I will be healed; save me and I will be saved, for You are the one I praise." (Jeremiah 17:14)

"Worship the LORD your God, and His blessing will be on your food and water. I will take away sickness from among you..." (Exodus 23:25)

"But I will restore you to health and heal your wounds,' declares the LORD." (Jeremiah 30:17)

"A cheerful heart is good medicine, but a crushed spirit dries up the bones." (Proverbs 17:22)

"Peace I leave with you; my peace I give you. I do not give to you as the world gives. Do not let your hearts be troubled and do not be afraid." (John 14:27)

"And the LORD will take away from thee all sickness, and will put none of the evil diseases of Egypt, which thou knowest, upon thee; but will lay them upon all them that hate thee." (Deuteronomy 7:15)

"Thou wilt keep him in perfect peace, whose mind is stayed on thee: because he trusteth in thee." (Isaiah 26:3-4)

"He gives strength to the weary and increases the power of the weak." (Isaiah 40:29)

"Then they cried to the LORD in their trouble, and He saved them from their distress. He sent out His word and healed them; He rescued them from the grave. Let them give thanks to the LORD for His unfailing love and His wonderful deeds for mankind." (Psalms 107:19-21)

"Bless the LORD, O my soul, and forget none of His benefits; who pardons all your iniquities, who heals all your diseases; who redeems your life from the pit, who crowns you with lovingkindness and compassion; who satisfies your years with good things, so that your youth is renewed like the eagle." (Psalms 103:1-5)

"The LORD protects and preserves them—they are counted among the blessed in the land; He does not give them over to the desire of their foes. The LORD sustains them on their sickbed and restores them from their bed of illness." (Psalms 41:2-3)

"He heals the brokenhearted and binds up their wounds." (Psalms 147:3)

"Who His own self bare our sins in His own body on the tree, that we, being dead to sins, should live unto righteousness: by whose stripes ye were healed." (1 Peter 2:24)

"Is anyone among you in trouble? Let them pray. Is anyone happy? Let them sing songs of praise. Is anyone among you sick? Let them call the elders of the church to pray over them and anoint them with oil in the name of the Lord. And the prayer offered in faith will make the sick person well; the Lord will raise them up. If they have sinned, they will be forgiven. Therefore confess your sins to each other and pray for each other so that you may be healed. The prayer of a righteous person is powerful and effective." (James 5:13-16)

What Can Hinder Healing in Your Life?

These things can stop your healing:

- **Unconfessed sin**
- **Failure to forgive others**
- **Bitterness in your heart against someone**
- **Anger**
- **Jealousy**
- **Hatred towards others**

• **Resentment**

• **Unbelief**

IT IS GOD'S WILL THAT YOU BE HEALED.

"Beloved, I wish above all things that thou mayest prosper and be in health, even as thy soul prospereth. For I rejoiced greatly when the brethren came and testified of the truth that is in thee, even as thou walkest in the truth." (3 John 1:2-4)

BE HEALED IN THE NAME OF JESUS. IN THE NAME OF JESUS, BE HEALED!

FOSTER CARE

As a retired Licensed Clinical Professional Counselor (LCPC), I have spent decades working with children and families, particularly in foster care, adoption, and trauma therapy. My experience at the Department of Children and Family Services (DCFS) for 28 years, Jackson Park Hospital for six years as a clinical therapist, and five years conducting play therapy for guardianship and adoptive families has given me profound insight into the struggles faced by children in the foster care system.

Children who have been part of the foster care system often experience profound pain, shame, and despair. Unfortunately, for some, foster care was just as traumatic—if not more so—than the environment they were removed from. Many children did not realize they needed to be rescued and did not understand the seriousness of their situation because it was the only life they had ever known. Some recognized their circumstances were different from their peers but feared the unknown more than the familiar hardships they endured.

To understand their experience, imagine living with your family and then, one day, being taken away by strangers. You may find yourself in a group home with other children, separated from your siblings, subjected to medical examinations, and asked a series of intrusive questions about your family. You no longer attend the same school, see your friends, or visit relatives. You are left with numerous unanswered questions:

• Have I been kidnapped?

• Did I do something wrong?

• Why can't I see my parents?□

• Where is my sibling?

• Who are these people?

• When will I go back home?

These children are often filled with anger, sadness, frustration, and despair. They may feel unworthy, unwanted, unloved—like "throwaway" children.

While some children, depending on age and maturity, understand the necessity of their removal and even feel relief, others have witnessed or endured horrific abuse and neglect. Many have been sexually abused, leading young girls to exhibit flirtatious behaviors and young boys to question their sexual identity due to their violations.

In high-profile cases of extreme abuse, children often still long to see their parents. Many display violent, destructive behaviors. Some have been suicidal, while others engage in self-harm, such as "cutting." Many struggle with extreme emotional distress, making residential placement necessary for their safety and the safety of their families.

If you are fostering a child, whether a relative or not, here are some steps you can take to help them:

- Patience, Patience, Patience—Show them unconditional love and ask God for wisdom in dealing with their trauma.

- Allow Them to Express Anger Constructively:

  - Write a letter to their abuser, read it together, then shred and discard it.

  - Role-play conversations with their abuser using an empty chair.

  - Use physical outlets like punching a pillow or a punching bag.

  - Encourage artistic expression through drawing their emotions.

At the end of counseling sessions, I have children repeat the following statement. You can print this out and encourage them to say it daily:

I cannot change what happened to me. It was never my fault. I cannot change who did not do what they were supposed to do for me. I will not let my past hold me hostage. I make a choice to forgive and move on. I have the strength and power to take charge of my life. I do not know what tomorrow holds, but I know who holds my tomorrow, and He holds my hand. I will live in the present moment. I trust God has a good plan for me as I step into my future.

Declarations Over Foster and Adoptive Children

- You are loved. (John 3:16)

- You are a blessing. (Psalm 127:3)

- You are special to God. (Psalm 127:3)

- You are blessed. (Mark 10:16)

- You shall be taught of the Lord and have peace. (Psalm 139:13)

- You have a special invitation to talk to Jesus. (Psalm 139:13)

- You have an angel watching over you. (Matthew 18:10; Psalm

91:11-12)

- You are obedient. (Matthew 18:10)

- You are wanted by Jesus. (Luke 18:16)

- You will not be ashamed of your youth. (1 Timothy 4:12)

- You are growing in wisdom and favor. (Luke 2:52)

- God is healing your broken heart. (Psalm 147:3)

- God hears you and will heal you. (Psalm 30:2)

- God can and will use your life for His glory. (1 Samuel 16-17; 2 Kings 22-23; John 6:9; Luke 2:41-52)

- God will anoint you. (Acts 2:17; Joel 2:28)

- You are not forgotten. (Isaiah 49:15; Deuteronomy 31:8; Psalm 44:21; Jeremiah 31:3)

- God is perfecting those things concerning you. (Psalm 138:8)

DECREES FOR MARRIAGE

SPEAK THE ANSWER, NOT THE PROBLEM.

THE ANSWER IS THE WORD OF GOD.

Heavenly Father, we come on behalf of couples and make these decrees over their lives:

- They will not put anyone before you. You will always be first in their lives.

- They will not lean to their own understanding but acknowledge you in all their ways.

- They shall be one, united in heart, mind, and spirit.

- Even as they become one, they allow each other to be who they are.

- The only thing they take from the past is the lessons learned.

- They shall never compare each other to anyone else.

- The flame of their love shall never grow cold.

- Each time they look into each other's eyes, they shall fall in love all over again.

- Laughter and joy fill their home.

- They kneel down as a couple to pray.

- They spend individual time in your presence.

- They understand that their first ministry is to each other and they do not neglect that ministry.[1]

- They make time for intimacy.[2]

- They spend quality, uninterrupted time together.[3]

- They allow each person to express their opinion and desires without judgment.

- They are anointed to love each other.

- Love covers multiple faults; no one is perfect.

- They are patient with each other as they walk together on this journey.

- Your wisdom rests upon those who are blending families.

- You bless their communication, and their words toward each other will be seasoned with grace.

- They never go to bed angry.[4]

- They do not use "blame statements" (e.g., "You always...", "You never...") but instead learn effective communication (e.g., "I feel like...", "I think...", "I wonder...").

- They face every challenge together with faith and courage.

- They recognize the truth of each other.[5]

- A threefold cord is not easily broken—God, and the couple. No one and nothing will come between them.[6]

I speak these blessings over their lives as I decree and declare: This marriage is blessed and not cursed. It shall flourish and grow stronger each day. Days shall turn into months, months into years, and years into a lifetime. Only until death shall they part. As an intercessor, I speak, decree, and declare it to be so, and IT SHALL BE SO IN THE NAME OF THE FATHER, SON, AND HOLY SPIRIT.

Note: I did not list the corresponding scriptures because you need to take the time to anoint yourself with oil, get quiet before God, and ask the Holy Spirit to assist you with writing decrees over your marriage. Do it individually, then come together as a couple to decree them over your life. Even if your mate, for whatever reason, is not a believer, guess what? You, as the family representative, have a legal right to decree and declare what thus says the Lord over your marriage.

---

1. For those in ministry, it is important to have proper priorities: God first, your mate second, even if you were already in ministry when you became one. You became one. The ministry comes next. Consult God if you don't believe this.

2. Intimacy ("in to me"): See me, hear me, talk to me, feel my heart, touch me, hold my hands, wrap your arms around me, tell me good things, speak well of me. There is a saying, "What it took to get them, it takes to keep them."

3. If there are children in the home, arrange for them to be elsewhere or go elsewhere yourselves. You deserve a night out or even a few hours. A date night does not include anyone else. While it is encouraged to be with other couples at times, it is IMPORTANT to have one-on-one time OFTEN. IF YOU ARE IN MINISTRY, PARTICULARLY AS A PASTOR, LEADER, OR SHEPHERD, IT IS CRUCIAL FOR YOU AND YOUR SPOUSE TO TAKE THIS TIME—TO VACATION UNINTERRUPTED (ONLY IF IT IS A MATTER OF LIFE AND DEATH). AS A LEADER, YOU MUST HAVE SOMEONE YOU CAN ENTRUST THE MINISTRY TO BRIEFLY. IF YOU DON'T BELIEVE ME, PLEASE CONSULT WITH THE HOLY SPIRIT. PERIOD.

4. Never go to bed angry. One of you may not wake up the next morning. How heavy of a burden would that be? To know your last words were spoken in anger. How much regret would you have to deal with?

5. In family counseling, I would ask the couple or family members to sit across from each other. Then I would ask them to describe what they saw from their seat. Afterward, I would have them switch seats and again describe what they saw. Then I would ask, "Do you feel they told the truth about what they saw?" You see, they were not trying to be unreasonable or difficult—it was their truth. Once you understand that it was their truth, how does that change your response?

6. Remember, when you are in ministry, everything about your life is a target for the enemy. The chaos and discord are not just about you. The enemy—the roaring lion—is seeking to destroy the ministry. Don't let him do it. Take a united stand against him and FIGHT FOR YOUR FAMILY. (Nehemiah 4:14)

RECOMMENDED READING

• *King James Bible*

• *For His Glory: Standing in the Gap—An Intercessory Instruction Manual* by Yvonne Perkins

• *Becoming an Intercessor* by Yvonne Perkins

• *How to Issue a Restraining Order Against Satan* by Vivian L. Harris

• *The Power of a Praying Wife* by Stormie Omartian

• *The Problems Facing a Pastor's Wife Today* by Ronald V. Ash

• *God Never Panics* by Nate Cater

• *Praying Prolific Prayers with Signatures of Prolific Women* by God First Ministries

• *God Encounters* by James W. Goll & Michal Ann Goll

• *Prayers That Break Curses* by John Eckhardt

- *Love: The Unfinished Chapter* by Dr. Prophet Laron Matthews

- *The Encounter with Wisdom: The Secret of Her* by Dr. Laron Matthews

- *New Season, New You: 40-Day Devotional for Women* by Jacqueline D. Marshall

- *Possessing the Gates of the Enemy* by Cindy Jacobs

www.ingramcontent.com/pod-product-compliance
Lightning Source LLC
Chambersburg PA
CBHW071729120626
46550CB00002B/451